Forward Fast

Forward Fast

Making Sense of Education in an Era of Rapid Change

Marc Isseks

ROWMAN & LITTLEFIELD
Lanham • Boulder • New York • London

Published by Rowman & Littlefield
An imprint of The Rowman & Littlefield Publishing Group, Inc.
4501 Forbes Boulevard, Suite 200, Lanham, Maryland 20706
www.rowman.com

6 Tinworth Street, London SE11 5AL

British Library Cataloguing in Publication Information Available

Library of Congress Cataloging-in-Publication Data is Available

ISBN 978-1-4758-4478-8 (clock : alk. paper)
ISBN 978-1-4758-4479-5 (paper : alk. paper)
ISBN 978-1-4758-4480-1 (electronic)

∞ ™ The paper used in this publication meets the minimum requirements of American
National Standard for Information Sciences Permanence of Paper for Printed Library
Materials, ANSI/NISO Z39.48-1992.

Printed in the United States of America

For Dad, my first and finest teacher.

Contents

Preface

My early days in the classroom were spent carefully writing exam questions on a master sheet, then patiently queuing up with colleagues until it was my turn to hand crank the mimeograph machine. Copying multipage exams all but guaranteed that I would be high by the end of my prep period. A little more than twenty years later, teachers and students can (soberly) exchange content through magical, invisible, wireless pathways—instantaneously.

Trying to grasp the rapidity of that kind of transformation is what sowed the seeds for this book. While living through technological revolutions is nothing new, people have never before been pushed to move so far forward this fast. The disruption to educational and societal norms has transcended nearly every aspect of our workflow, learning habits, interpersonal interactions, and creative expression. It's kind of a big deal.

As the world of education stands at this critical crossroads, it is worthwhile to examine where we have been and where we ought to be going. The technological tools of today not only give us an opportunity to enrich what we have always done, but they also provide fertile ground for exploration—inviting modern educators to rewrite the playbook on learning. It is in the spirit of inquiry, innovation, and breaking the rules that I have constructed these chapters.

To that end, I am a self-proclaimed *educational pyromaniac*—dedicated to lighting fires under educators who work and setting fire to systemic conventions that do not.

Therefore I invite all like-minded souls to give voice to their visions and help create engaging, inspiring, challenging, and compassionate institutions built upon the bedrock of ideas—the most powerful tool we have ever and will ever know.

Acknowledgments

Over the course of writing this book, a lifetime of school memories came roaring back—both as a student and professional educator. As those ghosts retreat to the recesses of my mind, it is not lost on me how privileged I have been to have known so many wonderful teachers, administrators, mentors, and students. Though abbreviated in this context, each word represents a million sentiments of gratitude.

Thank you, Saul Bruckner—your progressive vision of education forever altered the trajectory of my life. I owe a debt to Scott Martin, Robert Ellman, and Rory Schwartz for sharing their passion of the arts. Patrick Timpone, you gave me my first teaching job and therefore are to blame for all of this.

To my doctoral professors, Dr. Ryan Rish and Dr. Jo Yudess, your courses inspired two chapters of this book. Many thanks to the kind folks at the Hewlett-Woodmere Public Library for always finding an empty, quiet place for me to write.

To a quarter-century of professionals with whom I have had the good fortune of working, thank you for your patience, trust, and collegiality and for inspiring me to do my best on behalf of children. And to the thousands of young men and women I have met along the way, the lessons you have taught me line the pages of this manuscript.

A very special kudos to Nick Simone, a brilliant educator, a phenomenal sounding board, and a genuine friend.

To my editor, Tom Koerner, I am appreciative of the opportunity to write this book and sincerely hope that you do not regret sending me that email all those months ago. A big thanks to Emily Tuttle for her assistance as well.

I have been graced with a loving family, Andrea, Joe, Marc, Alison, Robin, and Scott, whose warmth, occasional craziness, and fantastic sense of humor keep me afloat. For the nieces and nephews who brighten my day,

Max, Jack, Lenni, Leah, and Tyler, it is my sincere hope that you have the good fortune to engage with school teachers from whom you learn to love learning.

To my mother-in-law Lois, thank you for always being so supportive and for not asking me to troubleshoot technology over the phone (fingers crossed).

For my mother Esley, I have boundless appreciation. Perhaps she knew then that letting her young son write on the chalkboard in her elementary classroom would inspire a career in the family business.

I also cherish the memories of two men who meant the world, my father-in-law, Mike, and my father, Edward, to whom this book is dedicated.

To my wife, Robin, whose excellence as a mother is unsurpassed and who graciously excused her binge-watching partner on many evenings so he could finish another chapter. There is no way this book could exist if it weren't for your extraordinary generosity and dedication to our family.

Last, for the two people who captured my whole heart from the instant I held them in my arms and who profoundly changed how I view the world, Sydney and Ian, you continue to make me wonder what good deeds I could ever have done to deserve you.

Introduction

This is no ordinary revolution.

Schools that believed the old adage "slow and steady wins the race" have come to the realization that they are getting lapped. In a forward fast world, technology waits for no one. Regardless of how we may feel about it, there is no longer any room in the teacher's lounge, principal's office, or Board of Education conference room for the complacent or the complainers.

This book is designed to take my fellow educators (and parents) to task by examining where we have been, how we got here, and what an effective school system of the future could (and should) look like.

Classroom instruction now competes against cell phones, its most formidable foe since the one-room schoolhouse appeared on the prairie more than a century and a half ago. To combat these agents of addiction, educators need to be more creative, collaborative, and courageous than ever.

This is a call to action for all educators, everywhere.

Yet despite what laypeople and technologists propose, zealously emptying district coffers to fill classrooms with an endless array of *our* gadgets to offset *their* gadgets will only muddy the present and endanger the future.

We must not just *use* technology, we must *infuse* technology to elevate the learning experience, develop critical thinkers, and unleash the enormous potential of our curious, talented, and passionate students.

The presence of technology alone will not win the day. Educators need to uncover ways to masterfully harness the power of digital communication, interactive applications, and an exponentially expanding mosaic, which intricately connects us all.

This kind of empowerment requires leadership built upon intelligence, intentionality, and insight. It also demands flexibility on a level never before experienced. In this exciting, albeit daunting, new era, educators who possess old-world knowledge of traditional methodologies and instructional skills from years of hard-won experience have never been more valuable. If we fail to bring these pillars of the past along, we do so at our students' peril.

This technological revolution has granted us the opportunity to imagine new worlds in which the previously inconceivable can become reality. It has also placed in its crosshairs the emotional well-being of young people, resulting from their inability to fully grasp the magnitude of social media and the high anxiety of living in self-imposed fishbowls.

For these reasons and more, the stakes for public education have never been higher. As we find ourselves engaged in a two-front war, with an increasingly globalized, educated populous exerting external pressure and internal forces seeking to weaken unions, while diverting much-needed public funds to profiteers with experimental schools of their own, we need respondents who are audacious, not tacit. It bears repeating: this is a call to action—time is of the essence.

What follows is a blueprint for how to move forward fast in ways that are wise, innovative, and motivating. The future is waiting.

Chapter One

Tech Graveyards

He likes trains.

This was the text we sent to all those who inquired about our son as he neared his sixth birthday. Grandparents, aunts, uncles, cousins, and friends were ecstatic to have this crucial piece of intelligence. First, it would make shopping a breeze. More importantly, it would ensure the gift would be well received. Who does not want to please a six year old?

The day finally arrived. We sang. He blew out the candles. Before I could finish spraining my wrist hacking up the Carvel cake that never had proper time to thaw, it began. Being smarter than his father, my six year old calculated that the cake wasn't going anywhere for a while, so he tore into his presents.

And there they were: curvy tracks, straight tracks, bumpy tracks, long cars, short cars, interlocking cars, conductor's hats, conductor's vests, little towns, big towns, viaducts, trees, crossing signs, more tracks, but no AA batteries of course (thanks, everybody). We had books on trains and pajamas and DVDs featuring Thomas the Tank Engine. If there were a scale to measure train saturation, he would have broken the meter.

Hour after hour we wrestled with packaging to break these toys free from their plastic prisons. The floor of his room morphed into Grand Central Station. No wrestling action figure was spared at least one ride. At long last, exhaustion set in, and our son passed out like a real conductor should: with his striped hat on. To make sure that he wouldn't trip during a middle-of-the-night bathroom run and because one of us is a neat freak (hint: it's not me), my wife and I converted a giant plastic tub into a toy train repository.

The next morning, we awoke to find him in the living room playing with a ZhuZhu Pet. "You want me to take out your trains?" I inquired. Barely looking up, he replied, "That's okay. I don't really like trains." And just like that, the Great Train Phase ended.

The next stop for these trains was the Toy Graveyard. ("Willoughby . . . next stop.") Every time I find myself in the school's basement I'm reminded of this story. That is our Tech Graveyard.

LIVING IN THE MORE AND NOW

When it comes to purchasing technology, school districts and six year olds share a lot in common. Often a product's life cycle goes something like this:

See it. Like it. Get it. Love it. Get more of it.
Find something new.
Grab the old. Visit the graveyard.
Forget the whole thing ever happened.

Of course, one could argue that the most obvious reason for this behavior in schools is the incredible pace with which technological tools evolve. After all, when a consumer walks out the front door of the Apple Store carrying the latest and greatest, even newer models are being delivered out back. In the past, Halley's Comet used to occur with the same frequency as the purchase of a new overhead projector, but these days it is a meteor shower of Proximas, laptops, desktops, tablets, SMART Boards, LED screens, Chromebooks, iPads, printers, cameras, etc. Just ask the administrator responsible for barcoding school property if we are moving forward fast.

Why is that?

Well, this phenomenon begins when the Board, superintendent, or principal likes something, sees something, or reads something and gets inspired to go out and grab a whole bunch of it. After all, if some of this stuff is good, then more of it must be better. Oh, and we need it now. Because if these tools are important in the future, they must be even more valuable right away. This is the Theory of Forced Perspective. It occurs when the person at the top of the food chain forces you to share his or her perspective.

Of course, acquiring all of this potentially valuable technology can be highly desirable and lead to many positive changes, but this breakneck rate of change does not come without a number of downsides. For starters, it is worth noting that in addition to being territorial and notorious hoarders (check those locked classroom closets and cabinets), educators also develop love-hate relationships with the technological tools they are forced, pardon, encouraged to adopt.

It is understandable for educators to demonstrate a modicum of hesitation provided the inordinate amount of time they must spend figuring out how to do all of the tasks they used to be able to do before they were given the new, shiny toy.

In a perfect world, educators would immediately recognize all of the wonderful benefits and instructional powers of their new devices or programs. They would then stop dead in their tracks and pivot to provide transformational opportunities for each and every student. In reality, the first step for teachers is to uncover how the new technology can be used to recreate the same old things they have been doing.

Once they find their footing, some teachers will eventually venture out and discover what is new and wonderful about the hardware or software in their possession. Then, and only then, will educators consider upending their worlds and either retrofit it or reimagine instruction to conform to the tech du jour. In other words, when you change a teacher's tools you knock their planet off of its axis temporarily. They do not typically appreciate that, but they will grow to forgive you . . . if your technology delivers on its promise.

However, when mandates, demands, and devices change too frequently, and a revolving door of platforms, applications, and protocols ensues, it can lead to technological nipple confusion. This breeds resentment and frustration (and a lot of crying). More importantly, very few people actually latch on. What follows is a self-fulfilling prophecy of technological unfulfillment. Ironically, this will frequently prompt leaders to seek out new technology that can solve the problems the old technology is failing to address. If only we had _____ now. Let's drop everything and go get it. Prep the graveyard!

This dog won't ever catch its tail. In a forward fast world, it is essential to acknowledge that a school's successes and failures will never be the result of the devices they use or don't use. There is something much more important, and it is the real revelation that drives change.

THE PHILOSOPHY OF HITTING

One of the lesser-known titles in the pantheon of sports-related movies is a little gem called *Max Dugan Returns*. It starred then-newcomer Matthew Broderick as the grandson of a con man on the lam, played by Jason Robards, who tries to reconnect with his estranged family before succumbing to the law, or possibly a terminal illness. After watching his grandson suffer mightily at the plate, Robards hires Chicago White Sox hitting coach—and swing guru—Charley Lau to correct his mechanics.

Whereas a present-day parent might opt to resolve this strikeout issue with a trip to Dick's Sporting Goods for batting gloves, an elbow brace, a helmet, stick 'em, Under Armour over-the-calf socks, cleats, and a $400 composite Louisville Slugger, Coach Lau tells the young ballplayer that they must begin by discussing "the philosophy of hitting." Of course, Broderick recoils quizzically at the premise.

Lau proceeds to explain the essentials: balance, transferring weight to generate leverage, and, most important, keeping your eye on the ball at all times. He reminds Broderick that you can't hit what you can't see. The pupil eventually finds success by implementing a set of precepts and letting those drive his approach. The audience leaves knowing that he will be able to incorporate these ideals in all facets of his life, as they transcend the act of hitting a baseball.

This helps explain why our schools have such expansive tech grave-yards—we often launch initiatives without first discussing the philosophy of hitting. We step in and take some pretty good hacks. Some may even make contact now and again. But we do not always have an approach that is reproducible or provides the stability that will generate repeated success over time. If educators find themselves with a streaming plethora of technological solutions, it probably means they never had a good philosophy to begin with.

Lest anyone need reminding, these tools aren't cheap. How many opportunities to create worthwhile educational experiences for kids were foregone to purchase yesterday's devices? Software? Textbooks? Accessories? Training? That's the fiscal danger of moving forward fast: we chase technology. Blink and your basement is a graveyard, filled with devalued relics of bad decisions past.

The giant technology companies aren't helping us either, as they build equipment that is designed for obsolescence. This is why schools should incorporate what technology they can, when they can, but only if it corresponds with a sound educational philosophy centered on challenging young people to think and develop a work ethic that will help ensure future success.

In the end, what students can do is far more valuable than what they know. This sets the stage for a very crucial debate.

Chapter Two

Content Is No Longer King

For as long as the American schoolhouse has existed, teachers were the gatekeepers of knowledge (perhaps second only to the local encyclopedia salesman). Educators stood atop Mount Info, armed with a master's degree in one hand and a dog-eared, not-so-recent edition of some publishing house's textbook in the other. They peered down from on high at the pubescent multitudes who sought their wisdom and, more realistically, a good grade.

In his Second Inaugural Address, our seventh president, William Henry Harrison, said it best: "Facts are important, and our nation's teachers know the facts; therefore, they are important."

Is that really true?

As a matter of fact, none of that is really true. Harrison, our eleventh president, was assassinated on the morning of his Second Inaugural Address.

Okay, that's also a lie. He was the ninth president and died just one month into his term because he didn't believe in winter coat technology. (Harrison succumbed to pneumonia, which he contracted giving his first and only Inaugural Address, though contrarian theories about his demise have recently surfaced—that is true!) Therefore there wasn't a Second Inaugural, nor can that vapid quote be attributed to Harrison or anyone else.

Does any of that really mean anything to you? If you only knew the first version of that story to be accurate, would it matter? The second? More importantly, you don't need a history teacher or her textbook to verify any of this. Simply say, "Hey Siri" or "Alexa, who was William Henry Harrison?"

Because of this seismic shift in how we obtain information, the immense knowledge teachers have spent a lifetime acquiring has suddenly gone the way of the owner's manual. It's still there and filled with lots of valuable stuff, but we do not rely on it anymore. Now when we need to deduce why the coffee grinds are dripping into the cup or the laptop refuses to boot up, we Google it. First and foremost, it is easier to find something online than in the junk drawer. This change in our learning habits goes way beyond digital copies versus paper. If we use Google to learn what ails our coffee maker and the first three hits are PDFs, we will probably cut bait and jump to YouTube (or click the "Videos" tab above the search bar).

The answer we seek may be right there in the first document, but we will still forego that selection and opt for what is more viscerally and aurally pleasing to us. It is irrational, diminishes our textual literacy skills, and may even cost us more time. Welcome to our new brains.

SHIFT THE GOAL POST

For educators who love content, this is the best of times and the worst of times. It is wonderful if they love to consume information; it's a nightmare if they are trying to teach it. The problem centers on a new reality, best encapsulated by Google's Chief Education Evangelist Jaime Casap, who acknowledged, "Facts are now a commodity." The marketplace has been flooded with nearly free, ubiquitous outlets of knowledge. To acquire new information no longer represents an ascension or achievement of any sort, nor does it impress anyone anymore. You too can possess that same information in just a few clicks.

Hey, you know something!

So what? More people have high school and college degrees than ever before and, thanks to globalization, the rising tide of know-how has lifted billions of ships. This means we can no longer delude ourselves into believing the myths of American educational exceptionalism. The intellectual and academic landmarks of yesteryear have been eradicated. In other words, emptying the public's coffers to maintain schools that are mere Fact Procurement Centers is poor stewardship of a nation's trust and treasure.

As we find ourselves deeper and deeper into this transitional phase of education, we need to ask ourselves some very difficult questions and entertain the possibility that we have a lot of challenging work ahead of us. Many districts are introducing tablets, often on a one-to-one basis. Are we merely looking to substitute pulp for kilobytes? Or are we striving to do something transformational? If it's the latter, then it might be time to examine the notes, documents, and PowerPoint presentations created before the technological revolution occurred.

In this new learning environment, perhaps it no longer makes sense to perpetuate the annual ritual of providing students with an array of facts and figures relating to a plethora of course content. To make matters more challenging, many of our assessments—especially on the state level—are centered on the content that students can recall from a week, a month, or a year's worth of learning.

This bizarre juxtaposition is akin to a joke by monotone comedian Steven Wright, who once quipped that he named his dog Stay. So when he calls his pet he says, "C'mere Stay. C'mere Stay." Handing out devices while keeping lessons and assessments nearly unchanged sends similarly mixed messages to our students. It also tacitly preserves an antiquated approach to instruction and learning on behalf of educators and children.

Like all things in nature, we respond to stimuli, commonly known in this business as mandates, directives, or standards. How educators respond to these stimuli is typically measured in assessment results, which drives how instruction is designed. A problem many of us face is that we are working very hard in the wrong direction. The game has changed. Content is no longer king. Therefore it is time to shift the goal post.

THE NEED FOR SPEED

People, especially the young, have undergone a revolutionary change in learning styles. Over the past two decades, humans, especially the young, have developed and strengthened a digital literacy that has outpaced textual literacy, quite simply due to a considerable amount of exposure to screens large and small. Imagine a person who goes to the gym seven days a week and does squats from Monday to Saturday. Even if Sunday is arms, chest, and shoulders, you are still looking at one oddly shaped person.

Thanks to dramatically increased screen time, our minds are becoming more and more like that—significantly out of proportion. And because the evolution of learning is moving forward fast, we are having difficulty modifying our instructional practices to adapt to this massive shift.

As a result of this rapid technological transition, schools are at a critical juncture. On one hand, educators know that meaningful learning occurs when everything slows down and we can navigate our students through a "deep dive." This strategy, which has traditionally centered on textual literacies, has worked very well for generations.

On the other hand, learning scientists recognize that the younger generation possesses an increased visual proficiency. Students are capable of consuming more information at a faster tempo. If you require evidence, look no further than a teenager zipping through social media apps on his or her phone. He or she is tapping, swiping, hearting, replying, liking, captioning, archiving, forwarding, and deleting at a breakneck pace.

These are not mindless acts. Each movement is part of a carefully orchestrated ritual to remain in the know while simultaneously maintaining or furthering one's status in a virtual society that has very practical consequences, often in real time. And this circus typically occurs simultaneously across multiple applications.

Therefore it is not unreasonable to conclude that many students who fail to demonstrate an understanding of facts while seated in the back of a classroom are not missing the boat because they are too slow—their minds are working too fast!

Centuries-old methods of spoon-feeding curricular content that have been subdivided by 180 school days, then broken down further into forty-minute, bite-size chunks is a pace so painful that some students prefer to check out. Much like getting stuck behind a senior citizen on a one-lane road in North Miami Beach (no disrespect, Grandpa), the lack of velocity could be enough to drive even the most enthusiastic driver to the point of surrender.

A smart person who isn't in a rush will wait until night, when the slower drivers are no longer out. Then he or she will zip back and forth, getting what he or she needs at a pace that is more satisfying. When we build classroom instruction around delivering content to a heterogeneous grouping of students over the course of ten months, we are putting many of them in cars on one-lane roads and, predictably, they disengage, get frustrated, or drop out.

Everyone knows the big secret—it's really easy to acquire information. That toothpaste is never going back in the tube. Students believe they can afford to update social media in class, then revisit the material later on and consume it at a speed that works for their individual tastes. It's not that content is devoid of importance, it just no longer holds enough value to warrant wasting precious time in order to procure it. Therefore educators should no longer misallocate classroom time solely delivering content, thereby foregoing learning opportunities of much greater meaning.

A better way to utilize time, while increasing the pace, is to introduce more multimedia elements into instructional practices. Video clips, pictures, memes, etc. are easily transportable and do not require traditional spaces to consume. In other words, students can get facts anywhere, anytime. Netflix and YouTube recognized this years ago and have prospered as a result of this transformation in content delivery. They discovered that a screen is a screen is a screen. Distribution need not require the television hanging on the wall in the living room or the desktop collecting dust atop the table in the den.

Educators would be wise to adapt in a similar manner. As consumers, we no longer want the items we consume to be presented in someone else's format or some artificial timeline. We want to binge. We want to hold content in the cloud, not in our hands. We want control over the process and to determine a timeline of our own. When "Must See TV Thursday" has been supplanted by "Netflix and Chill," we know that paradigms have shifted. Our propensity to desire information in a digital format is much greater than any other method of delivery. It's an On-Demand era and we are all coming of age together.

SLOW AND LOW, THAT IS THE TEMPO

Of course, rich educational experiences that permanently open minds and alter the directions of young lives cannot occur solely through a series of YouTube videos and Khan Academy clips. Like a sugar rush, these technological outlets provide fleeting hits of information, leaving one relatively satisfied in the short term but not nearly impacted enough for the future. The ability to think at the surface is not the ultimate goal of learning, nor is the objective to flitter around the web picking up little bits about this and that to consider oneself learned.

The web is incredibly proficient at telling us what we wish to know but often fails to inspire us or broaden our horizons. As a matter of fact, the algorithms that drive much of the web are sinisterly designed to steer us solely in the direction of that in which we have already demonstrated an interest.

Find a sweater, put it in your Amazon shopping cart, and watch how many ads for sweaters appear on your phone and computer over the next month. Machines can be taught to point a person in a different direction, but they aren't because it is not as profitable. Educators, on the other hand, desire nothing more than to inspire others to explore the unfamiliar and become intellectual risk takers. This is at the heart of what twenty-first-century learning ought to be about.

Our classrooms will thrive if we rely on *concepts* to drive our educational practices, rather than content. Concepts provide contextualization, which promotes deeper understandings and can fuel a student's lifelong desire to see what's around the next corner.

Shaping classrooms around the investigation of concepts offers fertile ground for research, sustained dialogue, and fostering an inquisitive mindset. This shift away from content should not only resonate within the structure of a typical forty-minute period but permeate through the courses we offer, the benchmarks we establish, and the way we structure the school day. We should strive to build learning environments in which the facts can come fast and the thinking happens slowly. For this to occur, consider following three pillars of making deeper meaning.

1. Motivation

After you have conducted a fair share of parent conferences, a pattern begins to emerge. You hear tale after tale from parents saddened by the notion that their children were once enthusiastic to learn way back in elementary school yet now appear uninspired, disengaged, and even apathetic throughout the secondary level. Essentially, children are falling out of love with learning.

Of course, there are numerous emotional and developmental changes that contribute to this metamorphosis, yet there are root causes that have nothing to do with hormones, pubic hair, or acne. First and foremost, studies show that students who have fallen behind in reading level by their mid- to late elementary years often fail to ever catch up. So they spend their middle and high school years climbing uphill while developing a deep resentment for learning.

Another culprit is that many students lose their fire because we inadvertently teach them to. We use phrases like "Work gets more serious now" and "Everything is going to be more difficult" as if these are inspirational slogans. Prior to secondary school—and, to a lesser degree, middle school—learning is masqueraded as fun. Students play games and sing songs; books and charts explode with color and illustrations. In other words, in the earlier grades we take great care to hide the peas in the mashed potatoes. When children get older, it's pretty much peas. All peas.

Wouldn't we be better off espousing how much more interesting or fascinating learning will become rather than bludgeoning young people with the least enticing aspects of growing up? By raising the bar with our choice of rhetoric, we could force ourselves to abandon the drudgery and monotony of a content-centric curriculum and deliver on lofty promises and heightened academic expectations.

Regrettably, there are educators who have developed a certain macabre *Groundhog Day*–esque sensibility in which the cycle of rote teaching to prepare students for low-yielding, poorly constructed, high-stakes assessments make us feel as though we're circling the hamster wheel in perpetuity. New year, same problems. Many have lost confidence in the ability of our leaders to establish meaningful, commonsensical, educationally sound policies. Spend five minutes in the teacher's lounge and you'll get an earful.

So what can we do to promote a stronger sense of motivation in our classrooms? For starters, we can get our mojo back—find ways to light our own fires in a grassroots way so that we may be able to conduct an Olympic-style torch relay with our students. Rediscover why we do what we do; recommit to taking the necessary measures to upgrade our skills and employ them with alacrity. Find like-minded colleagues with whom we can collaborate. Support the fight for appropriate standards, effective assessments, progressive learning methods, and fair wages—after all, this challenging and important work deserves appropriate compensation.

Second, we must fire out from the opening bell. A great launching off point would be to, once and for all, take the dreaded Do Now activity out back and treat it like a character who looked at Joe Pesci funny in a Scorsese film. Classroom lessons ought to begin with a motivational activity that challenges students to ponder an interesting thought, not review a fact, answer a test question, or spew back a definition.

In a world that moves forward fast, students require a compelling reason to put away their phones and tune out the drama. Starting a lesson with pure content reinforces the notion that nothing meaningful is happening yet. Remember, no one is paying a premium for facts anymore. That's hardly the tone we wish to establish. Students are not going to wait long before they find alternative curricula to consume their attention. Start with a "hook" and reel them in from the start.

A good motivation need only apply to the concept of the lesson, not the content. In many ways, something tangential makes for the best introduction because it will later provide opportunities for students to demonstrate an understanding by drawing connections and applying their learning in other contexts. Building those bridges provides an intrinsic satisfaction because it is derived from a person's skills, not what he or she has been directed to know. It tests students' abilities to put pieces together and expand their capacities. For most of us, that's incredibly rewarding. It ultimately makes us crave more. That's why motivation is a fire that needs to be lit.

2. Engagement

As if motivating students to learn isn't difficult enough, sustaining their engagement over the course of a class period is even more challenging. Now imagine keeping their interest for an entire school year. How about thirteen school years? Factor in the gravitational pull of technology, plus the socioeconomic issues that plague so many households, and you're looking at one heck of a daunting proposition. Dangling fancy papers called "diplomas" in front of kids offers a Later reward in a Now world.

These days the pace of life is so quick that delayed gratification is less and less common. There is, however, a secret to engagement that hides in plain sight. It has engaged people for millennia and casts a spell over us all. Inexplicably, we tend to overlook it, though we want nothing more than for our students to be completely rapt by the lessons we teach.

The secret ingredient: the power of narrative.

No matter how fast the world may move, people take time out for drama. Whether it be a great book, reality TV, or water cooler rumor mongering, we crave stories, innately and insatiably. A former writing teacher of mine, Doug Reed, once shared the formula for great storytelling. Reed said, "No obstacle, no conflict; no conflict, no drama; no drama, no story." If we intend our lessons to sustain student interest, they would be better served framed as minidramas. Within each discipline lies the opportunity to accomplish this.

Let's take a look at a fairly common science lesson on the father of genetics, Gregor Mendel. Science teachers typically introduce Mendel as a monk and a scientist who experimented with pea plants. A common Aim question might be: Who was Mendel? or What are Mendelian genetics? or How can we complete Punnett squares? or some compilation of these.

After the perfunctory background knowledge is passed along (with or without a picture of Mendel lifted from the first hit of an incredibly speedy Google search), the rest of the instructional period is spent defining terms like phenotype and genotype, then filling in Punnett squares.

Pause here for a moment and imagine the big picture from the child's perspective: There's a dead guy who tinkered with plants, which somehow explains why some people are tall and some people have red hair. Mildly interesting.

Is the period over yet?

Consider the myriad lost opportunities to bolster higher levels of engagement. From the bland, uninspiring Aim question to the rote learning activities, we are asking students to climb a rock wall made of ice. There's little to grab onto. Remember, no obstacle, no conflict; no conflict, no drama; no drama, no story. Granted, learning new terms can create an obstacle for the student, but the narrative tension ought to center on Mendel.

When the dramatic elements of his life and work are practically eliminated, it leaves our students with dry, decontextualized, relatively meaningless facts and figures. How can educators realistically expect high levels of engagement under these circumstances? Remember, there's a cell phone inches away with Snapchat streaks perilously close to being broken. Tick, tock, tick, tock.

Instructors would benefit from identifying where, in the story of Mendel, there are universally recognizable elements of the human condition. Where's the drama? Where's the conflict? Where's the human interest story? It is at these levels where we will get students to lean in.

Mendel was both a member of the scientific and religious communities, which were (and remain) endlessly at odds with one another. To what extent did Mendel's experiments contradict his own beliefs and values? When, throughout his years of experimentation, did Mendel fail and how did he overcome those setbacks? Were his findings immediately accepted and praised or did he have to go through a laborious process of deriving evidence to support his conclusions? Presenting learning through the dramatic lens of obstacle and conflict reinforces the challenges we all face in our lives. In that regard, Mendel's struggle becomes quite relatable.

A more engaging iteration of this lesson could include an investigation into the following:

1. What was Mendel trying to do?
2. What problems did he face along the way (both internally and externally)?
3. How did he overcome these obstacles?
4. How would you assess the way in which Mendel handled these situations?

Through this line of inquiry, we not only satisfy the curricular content, but we also achieve this by learning along *with* Mendel, not simply learning *about* Mendel. The lesson is transformed into a student-centered journey, filled with meaning and understanding—a far cry from checking another box in the scope and sequence guide and getting one day closer to the dreaded test.

More importantly, this approach reinforces invaluable lessons about determination and perseverance. Successful people often do not achieve their goals right away. That is the ultimate exercise in college and career readiness—it also explains why so many students return home from out-of-town colleges or drop out before they have earned degrees.

Last, educators will never increase engagement among students if they commit the cardinal sin of learning: watering down material. Content and concepts should be modified so they are appropriate for a student's grade and cognitive development but never stripped down to be made easy. Lowering the bar has the exact opposite effect of what one intends. Look no further than the games young people play in today's forward fast world. They are *unimaginably difficult!* Compare a PS4 controller to an Atari joystick. To call them both gaming devices is laughable.

Here's a premise for a first-gen digital game: Eat dots. Run from ghosts. Repeat at increasing speeds.

Compare that to the premise of a more modern game: Learn and master ninety maneuvers using a twenty-function controller. Complete a cost-benefit analysis of a multitude of rifles, light machine guns, and submachine guns. Develop a working knowledge of geopolitical conflicts, including a preexisting alliance system. Familiarize yourself with military jargon, types of armor, battle strategies, and how to save the game without going back to the beginning. Oh, and do all of this while collaborating with friends and strangers from around the globe in a densely complex virtual world.

Using the "water it down to make it more appealing" model of learning, we would assume that, if given the opportunity, young people would choose *Pac-Man* over *Call of Duty*. Nostalgia aside, that would never happen. Today's games are designed to take hours and hours to complete, requiring players to constantly demonstrate increasing proficiency in order to find success.

While certain elements become familiar, there are many unexpected twists and turns that keep a gamer engaged with the characters and the journey. These adventures are constructed around dramatic tension. Working through situations in which a player gets stuck adds to the fun, as there is a genuine interest and investment of time. The game never gets easier so a person can finish, one only receives helpful hints. That's not a coincidence.

Prolonged engagement occurs through a combination of interesting narrative and formidable challenges. It inspires people to work harder and overcome obstacles. By marrying content to skills development in an atmosphere fueled by the elements of great storytelling and setting high bars, we can make classrooms exciting while guaranteeing that students find the work to be hard. As Tom Hanks's character, Jimmy Dugan, said in *A League of Their Own*, "The hard is what makes it great."

3. Creation

In a biblical sense, everything begins with creation. However, in education, creation comes much later on. Students first must internalize concepts and content before they can demonstrate their understandings in any meaningful way. The most recent update of Bloom's Taxonomy supports this notion, as "Create" sits atop the new hierarchy, above all other cognitive skills. Not only does that make sense, it feels like the perfect response to how our world has rapidly evolved.

You don't need to go back too far to recall a time when the internet was shaped by large entities deciding the content that comprised the web. Barriers to entry were relatively high in the beginning as the brick-and-mortar world was transliterated into a digital medium. This was Web 1.0.

At the time, it felt like a seismic shift, but in retrospect it wasn't. The internet proved to be a super convenient place to go and get everything we desired, redefining how we consumed, not how we interacted. That all changed when we transitioned into Web 2.0.

Writer and reporter John Heilemann summed up this transformation best when he declared that "YouTube" supplanted "ThemTube." In other words, the world no longer waited for traditional content creators to fulfill their role. Armed with digital tools and nearly free distribution mechanisms, the democratization of information and entertainment marked a permanent change in how we absorb life. We don't only go to the web to get things anymore, we put things there as well. Creators are now consumers; consumers are now creators. In a forward fast world, lines get blurred pretty easily.

The desire among young people to both consume and create continues to grow exponentially. Like many aspects of life, this movement is motivated by power. Having a voice is power. Creation is power. By encouraging students to develop critical digital literacy skills through their own creativity, we will empower them to learn on the highest levels.

Training young people to create will better prepare them to tackle the rapidly evolving workplace. Today's employers want their workforce to be engines of ingenuity. They seek problem solvers, not subordinates requiring endless directives.

Teachers on the early childhood level come closest to shaping their learning environments around creation. Most days are filled with students making things to reflect their understanding of what was taught. No wonder elementary students tend to love school. They aren't grade conscious or slogging along because they need to satisfy a graduation requirement; they're having fun because their teachers are encouraging them to create!

While the children may receive stickers and stars for their efforts, those trinkets pale in comparison to the reward of seeing their creation hanging in the classroom or affixed to a bulletin board in a hallway. Even better is when work gets displayed on the coveted refrigerator door (especially at Grandma's house). It's a five year old's equivalent of hearing her song on the radio for the first time.

However, the extrinsic desire for one's work to be seen is not nearly as satisfying as the intrinsic value one derives from creating. It is from this inner desire that people are inspired to audition for a play, try out for a team, or sit alone at a computer for countless hours trying to write a book. We see the barren stage, the vacant field, and the blank page as places where we can create something unique, something personal, something larger than ourselves. It is where we can find our authentic voice.

That sense of risk taking needs to be nurtured in classrooms now more than ever. Creation evokes a sense of motivation and engagement. In the Information Age, nearly everyone can access the same content, but only a great teacher can remediate that content to give it new meaning in his or her own special way. A student's ability to create will help distinguish him or her in a highly competitive, globalized, and flat world in which content is no longer king.

Content is not the only collateral damage in this technological revolution.

Chapter Three

Burning Books

Florence, 1497

Multitudes of zealots, led by madman friar and virtual king Savonarola, participate in a "Bonfire of the Vanities" during which many works of art and literature that did not conform to the leader's single-story societal narrative were reduced to ash. It was a dangerous time for new thought, expression, and ticking off Pope Alexander VI.

This period illuminated (pardon the pun) how far people were willing to go in order to preserve traditional texts and their perceived meanings. Over five hundred years later, we find a new generation of people fired up (can't help myself) to burn down (it's too easy) past practices and chart a different course. Opposing them were stalwarts, willing to suffer mightily in order to preserve the world they once knew. It is a venerable passion play unfolding before our eyes.

Interestingly, one year after the pyres, Savonarola was hanged in Piazza della Signoria, outside of the Florentine political epicenter, Palazzo Vecchio. For emphasis (Italians have never been known for half-measures), his body was torched and whatever charred fragments remained were heaved into the Arno River. That is important to remember because unless both sides of the educational literacy issue find some common ground moving forward, it will end badly for someone.

Traditionalists deem literacy as a function of reading ability, comprehension skills, and language arts. For these individuals, texts are bound pieces of paper on which words are printed. This is lovingly referred to as literature. It is familiar. It is evergreen. It is sacred. But in a forward fast world, funny things happen to what is sacred. Just ask Savonarola.

It isn't that people stop being devout, they simply redirect their fanaticism elsewhere. And so traditional texts have suffered mightily in Information Age classrooms with the arrival of digital devices, both personal and school issued. Therein lies a major problem.

A number of telltale signs shine a solar-powered, LED spotlight on this seismic shift in literacy. First, the number of textbooks and novels that are returned to the school library in June that are in the same exact condition as they were when distributed in September has skyrocketed. There was a time when teachers required students to cover books because they were desperate to slow their wear and tear, ensuring their usability in the foreseeable future. Book cards had a place to mark the condition of a text, lest a child brought it back too worn, resulting in a fine.

These concepts are laughable now. How many books go directly in a student's locker or under his or her bed only to be unearthed ten months later? There's no need to protect them anymore; they will last an eternity under these conditions.

Second, take a trip to the average high school's English office. In many cases, the tenor is similar to the break room in the black-and-white TV sales department at Philco. What once was a hub of vitality and virility has been overrun by change, siphoning out the esprit de corps that used to fuel the swagger. The team knows exactly why their product is not selling but has taken an oath to extol the virtues of grayscales to anyone who will listen—or rather to those who are coerced by a rigid system of mandates requiring them to listen.

To make matters worse, so many high-stakes assessments are centered on English language arts, prompting teachers to run even faster and less productively 'round and 'round the hamster wheel. Additionally, these educators are exposed to increasing pressures from state leaders who have concocted inane accountability models tied to test scores and district administrators who bemoan low scores because they often yield the creation of remedial classes, which cost time, personnel, and materials—that's longhand for money, expected to come from nearly empty coffers.

Yet with all of this attention and the considerable resources deployed, results in reading and writing are abysmal. According to the 2015 National Assessment of Educational Progress (NAEP) exam, also known as the "Nation's Report Card," only two states in the union can boast that their eighth-grade students read at the *Proficient* level. Thirty-seven percent of twelfth graders are *Proficient*. Nearly one-third read at the *Basic* level, while 28 percent are below. Essentially three out of five "college-ready" young people do not read proficiently.

The results in writing are even worse. Slightly less than one-quarter of American eighth- and twelfth-grade students can write at the *Proficient* level. Blame could be placed squarely on the shoulders of social media, tweeting, texting, memes, and YouTube, but the fact remains that there is fierce competition for eyeballs now. This bell will not be unrung.

Like all other inflection points, educators must chart a course through this challenging time to ensure that they head in a direction that best serves the young people in their charge. To accomplish this, it may be time to set fire to books. Yes, that sounds drastic, but allow me to explain.

When systems move forward fast, food chains realign; hunters become prey. The behemoth Borders that once ate mom and pop bookstores for breakfast now lies in the belly of the beast called Amazon. In a similar vein, traditional texts—at one point the most powerful instrument of communication, inspiring revolutions and reformations—are, for the first time since Gutenberg, being abandoned by those who prefer multimodal content. It is difficult to blame them.

CONSTRAINTS AND AFFORDANCES

Compared to traditional texts, digital literacies come in an array of colors, so to speak. They appeal to users in ways that not only stimulate the mind but the senses as well, through sound, imagery, movement, and, yes, text. Of course, there is nothing wrong, per se, with traditional texts, just as there was nothing wrong with Henry Ford's Model T. It served the needs of a family at a price many could manage and was available, as Ford allegedly quipped, "in any color so long as it's black." Though that last part eventually became problematic.

Alfred P. Sloan, the head of a little startup known as General Motors, had the crazy idea that people may want to drive something a bit more personalized, so he sold cars in a range of hues. And so a new revolution in color began in the automotive industry, nearly destroying its manufacturing pioneer, Ford, in the process.

This upheaval was brought on by appealing to how a customer *feels* when consuming a car. It wasn't long before people bragged about the various trims and detailing that made their cars unique. The quest for expression has only grown over time. You can follow this trajectory all the way through to *Pimp My Ride*, arguably the pinnacle of automobile personalization.

People procure pleasure taking content that already exists and transforming it into something of their own design. We have long been familiar with the musical version of this: sampling and remixing. It can be as simple as taking your favorite ballads and making a mixtape for your significant other or grabbing the hook from an old Diana Ross song, adding a great beat, and laying down amazingly personal rhymes, like Biggie Smalls did. We are each finding our way toward fulfilling the beautiful and prophetic Sondheim lyric, "Anything you do, let it come from you, then it will be new." Such is the story of New Literacy Studies.

When the world went digital, and the tools to sample and remix became omnipresent, it triggered a dopamine tsunami that has grown stronger with each passing day. Spend one minute in a public space and watch how people interact with their phones (or look in the mirror). They are capturing multimedia elements—pictures, videos, sounds—and reconstructing them with text, emojis, filters, music, captions, images, etc. These creators are so proud of their work they proceed to share these new multimodal compositions with friends, family, and strangers. All of this creativity occurs instantly and incessantly.

Those on the receiving end analyze these texts using their newfound critical digital literacy skills. Each LOL and poop emoji changes the meaning of what they are seeing. Each sound, filter, and caption suggests something completely different and triggers a separate and unique visceral response. Back and forth, we interact with both familiar things in unfamiliar contexts and unfamiliar things in familiar contexts.

Each time we interact with and influence these texts, we make new meaning. More than the bells and whistles of cutting-edge technology, it is the satisfaction we derive from creation that truly compels us to engage in this behavior. In other words, it isn't so much what the technology does, it is what the technology allows us to do that matters most.

Hardline literacy traditionalists typically reject the validity of these multimodal digital compositions, claiming they are devoid of value or vapid. For the most part, they have a tremendous argument. The preponderance of the time people spend (young people, especially) creating and manipulating content is wasted because what they produce contributes very little to meaningful discourse or substantive academic pursuits.

It is safe to say that posting another cat video or political meme is overkill at this point. Yet most people are seemingly addicted to communicating in digital literacies. Regrettably, for adolescents, this frequently occurs in insipid, hurtful, or inconsiderate ways.

To oversimplify this problem, we can accuse young people of being lazy, disinterested, or incapable of "real" reading and comprehending by applying terms like *apathetic*, *alliterate*, or *illiterate*. While there are undoubtedly some students who fall into these categories, the lion's share of today's young people are actually "newliterate." They are not lazy in the least.

When it comes to consuming texts, the masses crave much, much more. All they want is to interact with and contribute to an ever-expanding global dialogue, which ceaselessly transpires in virtual spaces. One of our major shortcomings in schools is that we offer students too little to look at, too little to cognitively assess. The constraints of our texts are an immediate turnoff. Most adolescents have a voracious appetite; we are putting the wrong foods on their plate.

It is time for educators to have an adult conversation regarding the limitations of traditional texts. That need not suggest that this type of literature has diminished value in the pantheon of great artistic and philosophical expression; it simply means that there are new ways thoughts and ideas can be contextualized and articulated. Literacy has moved forward fast. An educator ignores that rapid development at his or her and his or her students' own peril.

GENIUS-LEVEL TALENT

Rapper, mogul, and fellow Brooklynite Jay-Z has frequently remarked, "Every human being has genius-level talent; you just need to find what you're good at and tap into it." While we can argue how to define *genius*, it is profoundly humbling to view education through the lens that we all have something special inside of us that needs to be nurtured and cultivated. This is an aspirational lens through which we can justify the school system's very existence.

Perhaps this is best experienced on the first day, when a teacher enters a room full of strangers, each with a story, each with a new chapter yet to be written. However, the way we actually approach education practically guarantees that schools will fail miserably at this inspirational objective. A deconstruction of an average language arts classroom will help shed some light as to why the road to uncover the genius-level talent is laden with roadblocks and landmines, mostly of our own design.

At some point in the opening days of school, the teacher distributes a novel selected by some curriculum team, school board, or, heaven forbid, state mandate. More than likely, it is chosen because the school already owns enough copies and acquiring a new title is cost prohibitive.

To quell their potentially less-than-enthusiastic responses, students are assured that this work is a "classic"—an essentially meaningless claim to neophyte readers. And by neophyte, we are essentially talking about most students under the age of eighteen. There are a small number who possess not only the verbal acuity but also the wisdom beyond their years to truly appreciate the axis-tilting power of literature. They do not comprise the majority of the student body.

To help ease the transition into this work of literature, many educators will attempt a variety of pre-reading lessons to help motivate learning, provide context, and build interest in the material. Often this includes some vocabulary work as well. These are laudable attempts to break down barriers and proactively build trust by establishing a covenant between adult and child: *I will guide you through and make this worth your time. Trust me.*

Then the books come out.

Immediately, the participants in this classroom experience a literacy disconnect. No matter how beautifully designed its cover may be, when a student opens a traditional text it is immediately unappealing for a number of reasons:

- it is black and white;
- nearly every page looks the same;
- it appeals to only one modality; and
- despite the introductory lessons, there are assuredly unfamiliar words somewhere, if not everywhere—another barrier to emotional and intellectual entry.

All of these roadblocks likely lead a young person to a simple conclusion: Abort! Granted, that oversimplification can frustrate adults. It smacks of your mother angrily asking, "How do you know you don't like broccoli until you try it?" Pushing away the plate is a child's defense mechanism to keep from venturing into a place of uncertainty, discontent, or something even worse. Let us also not discount the pre-adolescent and adolescent innate desire to *zig* when the adult commands a *zag*.

Furthermore, journeying into a traditional text is worrisome because there are many unfamiliar elements, so the perceived likelihood of failure is high. When the adolescent brain does a brief cost-benefit analysis, it is often determined that the risk is not worth the reward, if for no other reason than a young person does not even know what the reward is other than a passing grade. And to do something solely for a grade is a form of coercion, not engagement. That is no way to tap into genius-level talent.

To make matters more disconcerting, it is at this crossroad where we typically find the coercing of the coerced. Too frequently, language arts teachers do not necessarily love or desire teaching certain texts but are required to do so for several regrettable, yet realistic, reasons. So it is quite plausible that in a language arts classroom, there isn't a single person interested in reading a given text. Essentially, everyone has an extrinsic motivation to read—mainly fear of negative consequences—and no clear intrinsic inclination: love of art, pursuit of knowledge, becoming a more complete person.

In this scenario, the only person who has a way out of the literacy conundrum is the teacher. He or she is afforded an opportunity to create the lessons that correspond with the undesired text. He or she can bring together whichever additional elements he or she wants—traditional or multimodal. He or she can interact with the text in ways that satisfy his or her desire to create and make new meanings. He or she also does not have to concern him- or herself with simultaneously memorizing the stages of the Krebs Cycle, knowing the causes of the French and Indian War, conjugating irregular verbs, and applying the theorems, postulates, and properties found in proofs.

No wonder by the time the unit is over the teacher feels pretty good about teaching this book. He or she has found ways to infuse some of the affordances of critical digital literacies to better analyze, interface, and connect with the traditional text. However, that does not necessarily reflect the students' experiences.

For many students, receiving a so-called classic is akin to being forced to watch a black-and-white film. No doubt this sentiment is cringe-worthy to lovers of film, but there is a reason why multiplexes draw bigger crowds than arthouse theaters. I am not suggesting that blockbusters are better than independent or weightier films. However, if you are going to introduce someone to an art form, you will likely have greater success presenting material that is more accessible to their sensibilities at this particular rudimentary stage of their intellectual development. If you go straight to Ingmar Bergman, you may very well lose a future cinephile.

When emerging literacies were met with pre-digital literacies practices, a self-fulfilling prophecy was set in motion. Students were assigned traditional texts with too many constraints, which diminished interest in a substantive way. As a result, students failed to read the work as it was assigned. Originally, teachers resorted to punitive measures, like "pop quizzes," to help ensure that students did as they were instructed. To counter, students began using aides, such as CliffsNotes or SparkNotes, to feign understanding and dupe their teachers.

The adults quickly picked up on these schemes and created quizzes that were more and more specific, in an effort to be CliffsNotes proof. That all imploded when students finally surrendered and accepted their failing grades. This created a new problem for language arts educators: *How do I get these kids to pass?*

Therein lies an existential dilemma that exists when working with young people. Though we say our toolbox includes carrots and sticks, we really do not want to have to use the sticks because each whack potentially carries them further and further from ever wanting a carrot again.

So many educators went back to the drawing board and constructed a solution that is arguably worse than the original problem: if students will not read at home, we will read altogether in class. As a result, a typical language arts class can spend eight, ten, or twelve weeks reading a particular work. I cannot help but imagine what it would have been like to learn about my favorite childhood film, *Star Wars*, using this framework in my middle school English class.

(*Cue the dream segue music.*)

MRS. D'ANGELO: Good morning class. Today, we're going to watch the opening of a classic film.

CLASS: (*Audible sighs.*)

MRS. D'ANGELO: (*Turns lights off and cues a student, Marc, to start the reel-to-reel projector.*) This music is very famous. It was written by John Williams. He did a lot of movies with Steven Spielberg.

NOAH: Do we have to know that for the test?

MRS. D'ANGELO: No. (*Noah puts pencil down.*)

ADAM: Is this a Steven Spielberg movie?

MRS. D'ANGELO: No.

ADAM: (*Disappointed.*) Oh. (*Excited.*) Are we going to watch any Steven Spielberg movies?

MRS. D'ANGELO: He's not in the curriculum for this class.

ADAM: (*Disappointed.*) Oh.

MRS. D'ANGELO: (*Gestures toward screen—over that famous text scroll.*) Don't worry about the names of the different places mentioned here. It gets very confusing. Just know that there are different planets. (*Thinks better of it.*) Actually, this one is important. Tatooine. I may include it on the test. Write down, "Luke's hometown."

KAYLA: Who's Luke?

MRS. D'ANGELO: He's not in this part, but we'll meet him later in the week. Or maybe next Monday or Tuesday. I have to check my plans. Okay, pay close attention to this ship. I'm going to ask you questions about it. (*In the dark, she spots Sai Lai's raised hand.*) What?

SAI LAI: Can I go to the bathroom?

MRS. D'ANGELO: Is it an emergency?

SAI LAI: (*Hesitates.*) Yes.

MRS. D'ANGELO: Just know that you're responsible for anything that you miss.

SAI LAI: Okay. (*Takes the pass and heads to the courtyard to smoke a cigarette.*)

(*Mrs. D'Angelo signals Marc to shut the projector. She turns the lights on.*)

CLASS: Uh/Ow! (*Shield eyes from bright light.*)

MRS. D'ANGELO: That large ship is called an *Imperial Star Destroyer*. Using context clues, can anyone figure out what that means?

JACQUELINE: It destroys stars?

MRS. D'ANGELO: Maybe. . . . (*Searches for other hands.*) Maybe. . . . (*Finds a lone hand.*) Sandy?

SANDY: Doesn't *imperial* have to do something with government?

MRS. D'ANGELO: Good! Like?

SANDY: It's a government ship?

MRS. D'ANGELO: Good, we're getting it. . . . We're getting it. . . . And why do you think the *Imperial Star Destroyer* is so big? (*She nods in Anthony's direction and opens her eyes wide.*)

ANTHONY: It looked more long than big.

MRS. D'ANGELO: Well, I guess it's both.

ANTHONY: Is it longer than a football field?

MRS. D'ANGELO: Definitely.

ANTHONY: Wow.

MRS. D'ANGELO: Let's work off of what Anthony said. It's very long. Is it possible that's symbolism? (*Nods.*) Right? Marc?

MARC: Yes, it is.

MRS. D'ANGELO: Good! By the way, do you think one person can bring down something that big?

ANATOLY: No way.

MRS. D'ANGELO: (*To class.*) I think Anatoly is gonna be in for a big surprise in about three months. Back to the symbolism. What is the director telling us about this ship by making it sooooo big?

ANTHONY: It's more long than big.

(*Sai Lai enters.*)

MRS. D'ANGELO: Fine. What is the director telling us about this ship by making it soooo long?

SAI LAI: It's important.

MRS. D'ANGELO: Yes! Good job. Okay class, we'll continue watching the film tomorrow. Right now, take fifteen minutes and write about something important in your life.

SAI LAI: I forgot the pass. Can I go get it?

It is safe to say that had *Star Wars* been first presented to children in this manner they would have loathed it, not loved it. It is unnatural to watch this way, bordering on unholy. *Star Wars* is designed to be projected onto a flat surface at a rate of twenty-four frames per second, for approximately 120 consecutive minutes. Those are the constraints of the medium.

The filmmaker's affordances are the ability to fuse together light and sound in any method, sequence, manner, or form he or she wishes, including the utilization of visual and audio effects, to transform the viewer to worlds that never previously existed. More than that, the filmmaker gets to use all of those tools to make us *feel* something. Those feelings, more than anything, are what make it so meaningful.

Upon its first viewing, no film can withstand the scrutiny of being subdivided into sixty two-minute chunks, dissected over the course of a college football season. Someone who absolutely loves that film and has seen it dozens of times, however, might cherish the opportunity to engage in discourse over its meaning by delving into the minutiae. Not a first-timer. Yet this is how many novels are taught to neophyte readers with relatively underdeveloped cognitive skill sets and markedly unsophisticated tastes.

Unsurprisingly, students walk away from these works largely unimpressed and unmoved, if for no other reason than this "classic" was consumed incorrectly.

As those who enjoy reading will attest, there is nothing better than curling up with a good book. Once a great author sinks his or her talons into you, finishing pages becomes a form of intoxication. Hours melt off of the clock. Voice mails and texts go unreturned. Even social media is put on hold, a little. That says a lot about the power of reading for enjoyment, which occurs with extremely authentic levels of engagement. That sense of inebriation is your endocrine system's way of reminding you of the bliss we derive from intrinsic satisfaction.

This brings us back to the conundrum at hand. What are our intentions when we require children to read books over extended periods of time? Are we trying to promote the lifelong pleasure that reading can bring or the practical purpose of reading to accomplish tasks? If it is the latter, why aren't we filling our book closets with job applications, tax forms, mortgage statements, iTunes user agreements, food stamp regulations, military field manuals, Costco circulars, IKEA directions, Best Buy brochures, and other down-to-earth documents that will help our young people as they progress through the tangled red tape of life?

If our intention behind teaching children to read is pleasure and self-fulfillment, why are we taking so darn long to read a book? That isn't how real readers read. We do a terrible disservice to those students who enter our classrooms with a predisposed love of reading and those who may develop a similar fondness. Students face a catch-22 (though they have no clue what that is because the class has not gotten up to that part). The teacher genuinely and expertly motivates a child to read the "classic," but that child is chided for reading it too quickly.

If he or she ignores the teacher's warning and tears into the book, he or she may not remember the specifics when the exams come along in subsequent weeks. His or her teacher may infer that those poor assessments grades were the result of not reading—a truly nightmarish scenario for a conscientious student. Therefore it is safer to punt and read it in class with everyone else.

You can identify the students experiencing these dilemmas as they are the ones strolling around the halls or sitting in school libraries with books of their own choosing. And they will typically finish several books before the class polishes off that "classic." Once more, we observe how powerful grade coercion can be, modifying behavior in ways that push against increasing and sustaining high levels of engagement.

This brings us back to the adult conversation many school faculties and departments of education need to be having. In a forward fast world, educators and educational leaders have to ask themselves this series of critical questions:

1. Is the literature that we are selecting knowingly or unknowingly promoting a single story narrative? In other words, are most of the authors speaking with one particular voice (that is, writing from a Western Hemisphere perspective)?

Single story narratives do not jive well with New Literacy Studies. The internet has connected us in ways that were unimaginable when many curricula were created and book purchase orders were approved by the local school board.

When you examine the Common Core Learning Standards for English Language Arts 6–12, you find that most recommended authors are male and a preponderance of the works were produced over one hundred years ago. Those should be red flags. Leaving comfort zones and exploring new voices is imperative if we are going to cast the widest net possible to captivate students and pass on the immense value of literature.

2. How do we handle the "Bard situation?"

This is a tough one because so many hold the works of Shakespeare in the highest regard, and understandably so. Yet we would be hard pressed to find an author whose name is more synonymous with dread and more off putting to middle and high school students than the genius considered to be the finest dramatist in the history of the world.

To Bard, or not to Bard?

Perhaps it is easier to begin with what we should not be doing. When we factor in the complexity of the language and the reality that only one-third of high school seniors read at the *Proficient* level, it seems a comedy of errors to make Shakespeare a requirement. Rather, reading his plays should be the reward for which we strive.

It comes across a bit paradoxical to hear his diehard defenders argue that Shakespeare is timeless and universally appealing, yet to get students to read his works they must be required. If his work is brilliant and perpetually relevant (which I would argue it is), young people who have been trained and inspired to love literature will find their way to great writing throughout their schooling or, more importantly, over the course of a lifetime.

The flipside is coercion, which often morphs into marching countless hordes through works that they do not understand, appreciate, or ever wish to revisit. When the deed is done, we can claim to have passed along the great tradition of Western literature.

Is that how classics have stood the test of time?

It cannot be that these works were mandated because attending school was not even mandated for nearly three hundred years after Shakespeare's death. Yet they continually found an audience.

If there is one universal truth about Shakespeare—or works by any great artist—it is that you absolutely must go back and revisit their creations to maximize the emotional and intellectual impact. No matter how slowly a teacher proceeds through *Hamlet*, students will walk away with a superficial understanding at best because it possesses layers that can take a lifetime to unpack. Therefore taking one's time with Shakespeare violates the *law of diminishing marginal productivity*, better known by its street name, the *law of diminishing returns*.

Essentially, there is only so much that we can expect students to reasonably absorb from any piece of literature, especially Shakespeare. Once we reach that level, every minute thereafter could be better spent doing something else. So if you are going to introduce Shakespeare in the classroom, do it quickly. If they hate it, it's over soon. If they love it, they can reread it for the rest of their lives.

Furthermore, educators will increase student engagement, as well as independent reading, by challenging students to perform Shakespeare. This goes well beyond randomly assigning roles each day in class and reciting the text aloud. In order to take advantage of critical digital literacies, students must be afforded the opportunity to make meaning of Shakespeare by utilizing whichever tools they feel most comfortable to demonstrate their understanding. Their performance should be multimodal, not only aural.

Maybe students want to record and/or edit a video to explore the relationship between Hamlet and his mother. Perhaps a student prefers to take a picture of Kenneth Branagh as Hamlet and use Instagram filters to convey his mood during a pivotal scene. Or another student may wish to create a digital photo essay capturing the theme of betrayal or vengeance. By sticking to the biggest concepts and most overt themes, educators can make Shakespeare feel incredibly accessible. Expressing an understanding in a multitude of ways promotes individuality, heterogeneity, and the evisceration of the single-story narrative—there are myriad ways to interpret art.

This also serves another important purpose. We dedicate a tremendous amount of time teaching young people how to interpret and analyze the voice of others, but how often do we ask them to explore their own voices? When do we challenge them to establish an identity with their work? Granted, most will have great difficulty differentiating themselves at first. But over time they will discover ways to put their personal stamp on what they produce. And when students cross that threshold, they will unlock a whole new appreciation for the authorial voices found in the literature they are reading.

Another way to incorporate new literacy studies is to promote reading through visuals. To some extent, watching the film adaptation of a novel or play helps, but the language can still present problems. These obstacles may be transcended with graphic novels and digital storytelling. Opening such a work immediately alleviates students' trepidations regarding text, language, and vocabulary deficiencies. Once freed from these perceived (or actual) weaknesses, they can be guided through an analytical exploration of characterization, imagery, symbolism, and every other critical aspect of language arts that are stressed in classrooms.

Consider challenging students to write their own dialogue to accompany the images and discuss how the text impacts the visuals. Furthermore, seeing different examples of text over images will promote higher-order thinking skills as students debate how each provides different meaning to the story and its characters. These are skills they are already practicing through their nonstop interactions on the internet. Meaning making promotes agency and taking agency is critical to advancing engagement.

Teaching literature in this way, however, may mean casting aside some of those beautiful but baffling couplets or countless examples of symbolism, imagery, and subtextual elements that raise the barrier to entry and keep students at arm's length. The alternative is to give Shakespeare his hour upon the stage and then be heard from no more.

3. Is literacy an English-only endeavor?

All too often, reading and writing are left to language arts educators. Students hear quips like, "You don't have to worry about grammar/structure/reading/writing, this isn't English class." This puts language arts teachers at a tremendous disadvantage because they typically see students for only one-eighth of the school day. What educators of other disciplines fail to recognize is that by not echoing the new literacy strategies and methods promoted in language arts classrooms, students are far less capable of demonstrating proficiency in other subject areas as well.

As we know from the changing formats on national and state assessments, less and less emphasis is being placed on the low-level regurgitation of facts, definitions, and memorization. In an effort to raise the academic bar, students are now tasked with analyzing, comparing, explaining, and demonstrating other cognitive skills to produce satisfactory, in-depth responses to examination prompts.

If students are going to be tested this way across disciplines, it is therefore incumbent upon all educators, regardless of subject area expertise, to challenge pupils to go beyond the curricular content and promote literacy skills. Only when a school's faculty adopts a similar mindset will it enjoy the benefits of the Tanzanian proverb *many hands make light work*.

ARCHIMEDES, *PRINCIPAL*

As the great mathematician, philosopher, and all-around smart guy Archimedes once said, "Give me a lever long enough and a fulcrum on which to place it, and I shall move the world." The lever that educators, especially in language arts, have been pining for is literally right beneath their students' noses. By leveraging young people's love of digital literacies, we can inspire newliterate readers to, slowly, over time, become lovers of all sorts of great literature.

First, however, district and school leaders must be brave enough to set our traditional texts on fire in order to take advantage of the affordances offered by technology. If they are successful, those flames will rekindle a new generation's fondness and appreciation of reading.

Schools will produce multitudes capable of taking greater agency in their learning and exchanging ideas with a robust, multicultural perspective. Students will come to understand the plain truth about language arts: reading is all about rereading; writing is all about rewriting. Typical learners do not "get it" the first time around. However, when people persevere, they unlock their fullest potential to do extraordinary things, like tapping into genius-level talent.

Let us forego the mandates on literature and replace them with a directive to promote thinking each and every day, no matter what. Whenever we hear students profess, "I don't know what to write," what they are really saying is, "I don't know how to think, therefore, I'm unable to demonstrate any understanding of this prompt." By promoting creativity through digital literacy practices, we will get far closer to our goal of having students who can communicate using the written word. There is very little downside to employing these strategies right now because the majority of students are not reading and writing anyway.

While we are making bold, radical changes, perhaps we will consider not grading students based on their ability or willingness to read what the adults have mandated. Rather, let us assess students based on how they perform, create, and make new meanings with the knowledge they are acquiring. Becoming an educated being is a lifelong, active pursuit, not a tacit exercise requiring thirteen ten-month segments to complete.

A NEW BONFIRE

From the embers of Savonarola arose eras of great thinking, reading, and writing: the Renaissance, the Scientific Revolution, the Enlightenment. In each, communities chose to abandon the single story of the time, in exchange for a more open, multiperspective view of the world. It was far from perfect, but far better than what previously existed. We have the opportunity to stand on the shoulders of greats and carve our own unique path into the future, but it will involve seriously rethinking and retooling how we define *literature*, *classics*, and our approach to teaching them.

Audiophiles have come back to records. Cinephiles warmly embrace black and white. It may very well be that the way back to traditional literature is through new literacies, but first we need educators brave enough to light the match.

Chapter Four

The Reese's Peanut Butter Cup Theory of Edu-Technical Synthesis

Premise: Lots of veteran teachers have pedagogical skills.

Lots of neophytes have computer skills.

Problem: Who bridges the gap?

Further Problem: Does a causal relationship exist between technology and learning? (Hint: Don't ask Apple or Google.)

One of the most significant disconnects that schools experience is the divide—occasionally a chasm—between the past and the future. Members of these two camps typically collide on a number of battlegrounds, including professional development, classroom instruction, and budget. It's fairly easy to identify each group by the language they use. For example, "I remember when we . . ." or "We've always done it this way . . ." are clearly members of the "We've been here and know a thing or two" contingency.

Then there's the "What if we . . ." or "There's an app for that . . ." group, who don't necessarily have the experience or battle scars of their more seasoned colleagues but possess a willingness to explore new possibilities. Each faction brings considerable talents to the table, but alone, neither group is capable of providing twenty-first-century learners with the full panoply of skills needed to maximize their potential.

Think of it this way: one is peddling peanut butter and the other is parading around with chocolate. What we need is for one of those happy accidents, which frequently occurred in Reese's commercials. For those with enough years on this planet to recall, a typical ad would feature two klutzes, each carrying his respective treat. They would inevitably collide, landing one person's food in the other's.

At first, both sides appeared quite annoyed—borderline horrified—that their snack was disrupted by that dastardly insensitive and highly uncoordinated other. "Your chocolate is in my peanut butter," one would decry, prompting the other to fire back, "No, your peanut butter is in my chocolate." It wasn't until they each took a taste that an epiphany occurred and, ultimately, so did reconciliation.

We are at a similar moment in education.

"Your device is in my classroom."

"No, your classroom is in my device."

Neither group of hardliners appears happy to welcome in the other side. We are experiencing this disconnect in part because we've moved forward fast and there has been very little time for acceptance or the necessary bridge building. In other words, many have yet to really taste what this new combination is like. It isn't from a lack of trying, but many schools are going about making an educational peanut butter cup all wrong.

Anyone who has ever tried Reese's signature candy knows that this isn't produced through a simple collision of two relatively unhealthy yet really delectable ingredients. However, this oversimplification is often at the foundation of how technology is incorrectly incorporated into the classroom. This misstep can be attributed to educational leaders who frequently ask the wrong question of their teachers. Rather than inquire *if* someone is using technology, it is critical to ask *how*. However, there is a "Hierarchy of How" (HoH) that shouldn't be overlooked.

At the lowest level of HoH all educators are taught the essentials. This is a time for professional development regarding logins, settings, hardware, and software. A common pitfall that occurs during this phase of the hierarchical progression comes from a failure to recognize the many different levels of comfort, understanding, and growing expertise faculty members have regarding digital technology. Working with so many disparate skill levels makes meeting everyone's needs (that is, pleasing them) incredibly challenging.

The fastest way to turn someone off is by requiring him or her to waste time relearning a technological skill he or she has already acquired. Equally maddening is exposing a techno-neophyte or technophobe to more than he or she can comprehend at a given time. This kind of training makes people contemplate early retirement or joining a traveling circus. In a way, educators are like Goldilocks—they need their professional development to be just right.

The second level of HoH features an introduction to the tools through which collaboration can occur in digital or virtual spaces. In this phase, an emphasis should be placed on clouds, apps, sharing, and thinking beyond the four classroom walls. Once again, it is imperative to be mindful of how many different levels of understanding and expertise there can be at this stage.

It is equally important to embrace the reality that as our professional workshops on these tools are taking place, companies, ranging from multinationals to dorm room startups, are supplanting these applications in real time. The status quo no longer hovers. It took the Renaissance one hundred years to move from Florence to London. Now seismic shifts happen in an instant (#renaissance).

This is why the progression through the HoH must be underscored by the constant reminder that, from this moment on, everything remains in a state of flux, permanently subject to revolution or insurrection. Long gone are the days of writing one's lesson on a white piece of paper and utilizing it until the sheet turns yellow, asserting that if it was good then it'll be good now. For some, this will come as no surprise, but for others, it will be the source of tremendous trepidation and, possibly, a touch of animus.

Arguably, the reason we have yet to harness the true power of smart technologies in many of our schools stems from a failure to move beyond stages one and two of the hierarchy. For a number of educational leaders, the implementation phase ends with the delivery of hardware and software. For others it concludes with training on apps, clouds, collaboration, and virtual classrooms.

When these bosses walk around school buildings and see devices on each student's desk, they spike the football and do their touchdown dance in front of the Board of Education or whoever may have hired them and approved those huge expenditures on technology. Anybody can spend money, but the best purchases are the ones that maximize value—a sentiment frequently overlooked.

Perhaps the reason most leaders are easily mistaken is because at stage two the tech giants descend upon the school district. The gurus from Apple or Google descend from Mount Silicon to certify teachers and administrators, donning each with the Technologists' Medal of Honor, the Valley's highest accolade.

Then, like Professor Harold Hill, the salesman/con artist from *The Music Man*, they are on to the next town, leaving behind a treasure trove of expensive instruments that few really know how to play—but the townspeople's self-esteem is through the roof because they have been made to feel like part of something special.

When pressed by the town contrarian, Marian the librarian, to demonstrate how people without a musical background can produce beautiful sounds with these new instruments, Hill employs the "Think Method." He asserts that if you think about the notes, you can play them.

This is the same empty, faith-based methodology Big Tech gurus provide. "If you use our technology in school, children will learn more." Like the folks of River City who gush at the sight of their kids in marching band uniforms long enough to let Professor Hill skip out of town, our schools and communities are so swept up in the 1:1 movement that few have stopped to ask if there's any evidence to support the claim that these devices help raise student achievement. Of course, the salespeople provide ample assurances, but here is the stark reality: Technologists are not educators.

It bears repeating. Technologists are not educators.

Apple and Google are not in the business of developing young minds. They are in the business of developing addictions, from which they will derive perennial fortunes and increase shareholder value. Undoubtedly they excel at designing and manufacturing incredible products that offer so many wonderful capabilities. Therefore they are entitled to enjoy windfall profits for their extraordinary efforts. Regardless, it does not make them educators.

The promise of "a device on every desk" will not improve what ails twenty-first-century education any more than "a chicken in every pot" ushered in American prosperity in the months leading up to the Great Depression. Frankly, the sight of these devices is as meaningless as eyeing a pencil, paper, or an abacus—just a whole lot more expensive.

Education and technology have to be blended together in the right proportion for it to be the solution that everyone craves. Implementation and utilization should be rooted in the best educational practices, with an emphasis on augmenting the theories of learning that form the neural network of schooling to produce something entirely new yet with many recognizable elements.

This premise is at the core of what the food scientists at the Reese's kitchen were able to achieve with their peanut butter cup. Benefitting from decades of research, along with countless taste and marketing tests, the chemists and cooks unlocked a formula that synthesized the familiar while creating something brand new. For the parent company, Hershey, these trials came at a nominal cost. In the world of education, experimentation comes at a much steeper price.

Not only does hardware cost a fortune relative to typical school budgets, but, more importantly, every time leaders make the wrong calculation or attempt a well-intentioned but erroneous initiative, they risk providing our young people with crucial skills and knowledge. In the learning business, there aren't any do-overs. Once students pass through, they will never come our way again.

Because of these incredibly high stakes, some educators will politely cast their devices aside and rely on their bread and butter—tried and true instructional strategies. This may be viewed as rigidity or reluctance to change, but it comes from a very real and honorable place. That is why the third stage of the HoH is the most critical. It's where Big Tech meets human capital: *edutechnical synthesizers*.

Most major industries have synthesizers: people who combine the best of two worlds and produce something that never could have existed before. The great filmmaker Robert Zemeckis is a wonderful example of a cine-technical synthesizer. In his masterwork, *Forrest Gump*, Zemeckis seamlessly wedded computer-generated special effects shots into a personal story about a man from Greenbow, Alabama, with a developmental disorder. Zemeckis weaves his technical wizardry into a story that could not exist in that incarnation without it.

The canvas on which he paints is vaster, allowing us to take a far-reaching journey that concludes with an intensely emotional payoff. Story does not exist to serve the special effects, as we might find in any number of films centered on alien invasions and the destruction of major cities. Rather, Zemeckis valued the idea that technology must service the story.

Focusing on the heart and mind while integrating sights and sounds that are pleasing to the eyes and ears is at the essence of what we expect from a synthesizer. This isn't easy to come across because it requires innovation, passion, imagination, and absolute expertise in one's field. However, it's exactly what we need in education right now.

The first generation of edu-technical synthesizers, like all pioneers, faces incredible challenges. Their sod busting will involve breaking through the defensive walls constructed by the fearsome and the nonbelievers. Furthermore, there is presently a dearth of substantial research validating the notion that web-enabled devices increases student achievement.

Frankly, this first wave of data ought to be taken with a mountain of salt because we have yet to properly implement the technology into most classrooms. Simply placing an iPad in a student's hand will not improve learning any more than putting a biology textbook under your pillow will help you understand photosynthesis.

Synthesizers will need the fortitude to stand up to those who proclaim that life was better back in the old days of chalk and erasers. They will also need to turn a deaf ear to the Board member or superintendent who demands that implementation be expedited without any real regard for the instructional consequences.

Indeed, these are trying times for synthesizers, so they ought to be a special lot. They must not only possess the vision of constructing castles in the clouds but also know how to requisition the materials and engender the goodwill necessary to build the ladders and embolden everyone to begin the climb.

True synthesizers recognize that teachers who are directed to do something will typically respond with mere compliance, while those who are inspired frequently become evangelists. In this regard, they are very much like our students. Perhaps the greatest feat will be to convince the masses how to think as synthesizers. This means training them not to confuse bells and whistles with meaningful instruction. Because something is done through an app, on the web, or using a device does not mean it is an effective use of technology (that is, aliens blowing up the White House).

Like the mighty samurai and brave knights of centuries past, synthesizers live by a code too:

1. Technology must service learning, not vice versa.
2. Respect people's fears and resistance by listening to what concerns them, then build from a place of compassion and understanding.
3. Throwing everyone in the deep end of the pool does not promote technological proficiency, it promotes drowning.
4. Specificity matters: no one cares why tech is good for everybody; they only care why tech is good for them.
5. Sometimes the technological solution is not the most effective one; don't be afraid to kick it old school.

The technological landscape in schools is undergoing its greatest and most rapid shift ever. If we don't pause ever so briefly to muster the courage and construct some new value systems, we run the risk of being overwhelmed by change. However, if synthesizers can help institute new precepts, we will be able to harness the power of this revolution, reap the rewards, and make peanut butter cups that will satisfy the masses.

But first we must overcome one tiny obstacle.

Chapter Five

The Irony of Thumbs

Humans are relatively slow and weak and they do not climb particularly well. They cannot fly, leap, or stay under water for very long. Considering the majesty of the animal kingdom, with all of its physically spectacular and awe-inspiring traits, *Homo sapiens* should have been kicked to the evolutionary curb a long time ago. However, they possess one short, stubby digit on each hand that slightly faces the other four, which has proven to be their competitive advantage over all other living things. Millions of years later, these opposable thumbs are proving to be the greatest threat to the social fabric since Paleolithic people first painted emojis on cave walls.

About twenty years ago, when the internet became a staple in most households, chat rooms abounded. It didn't take long for these social encounters to devolve into breeding grounds for lascivious behavior, including cybersex. Had these prurient interactions remained among consenting adults that would have been fine, though a waste of humanity-changing technological innovation. However, deviants with a penchant for sexualizing minors quickly discovered that they could digitally disguise themselves as young boys and girls, then seek out deplorable trysts.

In a flash, television shows were dedicated to catching these predators. Parents recoiled at the notion of a forty-something pervert (almost always male) using his laptop as a Trojan horse to sneak, undetected, into their homes. Like most aspects of the Information Age, this evolved quickly. And while some of these monsters undoubtedly still roam cyberspace and gaming networks trolling for their next victim, they are no longer the primary threat to young people online.

The good news is that this new threat does not pretend to be someone it is not. It does not try to lure unsuspecting children into unmarked vans, nor is it very sophisticated. As a matter of fact, this new threat probably does not even have a license to operate a vehicle of any kind. The bad news: it's your neighbor's kid. Or the kid across the street. Or the kid two blocks down.

Worse yet, the greatest threat to the children in your community may in fact be the kid who lives under your roof. No matter which child it is, rest assured that he or she attends your neighborhood school.

SMART PHONES, DUMB PARENTS

At the root of this problem is a misconception common among many parents. They erroneously believe that when they bestow a child with a cellular device, they are handing over a phone. However, smartphones are not phones. True, they look somewhat like phones because there is a speaker to hold up to your ear and a mic into which you can speak.

The manufacturer calls it a phone. The receipt even has the word "phone" printed there, but this is a gross oversimplification. The folks on Noah's ark did not experience "rain," they endured a cataclysmic event (aka the Wrath of God). To that end, the package that houses your child's "phone" should read: *The Most Powerful Thing Anyone Your Age Has Ever Held in the History of Humankind.*

Furthermore, it should include the following warning for parents:

> *This handheld computing device offers unfettered access to the internet, through which your child can learn about the Revolutionary War or how to build a bomb using cleaning supplies found in your kitchen or chat with a friend or bully someone until he or she contemplates suicide or play mindless videogames or becomes a more informed citizen of the world or buy things with your credit card (sometimes without even knowing) or video conference with grandma (who misses him or her so dearly since he or she moved away) or watch porn, so much porn, miles and miles of porn (if that's how porn is measured).*
>
> *Pretend this box contains a chainsaw. Would you just hand it to your child without reviewing at least a few safety tips?? (Seriously, would you?)*
>
> *Active parental supervision is advised (required).*

Perhaps if smartphones were marked accordingly, parents would give them the attention they deserve. But they are not, so, inexplicably, they do not. A forward fast world has a way of making you pay mightily for your naiveté.

Frequently, paranoid parents, who claim they understand mobile technology, justify their purchases under the guise of safety and convenience. They assert that they want peace of mind in knowing their child has made it to practice, has enough money for a snack, or is ready to be picked up. These objectives seem innocuous enough, but there's a larger problem at play.

A smartphone is a disproportionate tool for the relatively nominal wants and needs parents proclaim to have. If you want to remove a splinter from your big toe, you could amputate the entire leg, which certainly would resolve your thorn issue. However, that is way too much response for such a small problem. True, the splinter would be gone, but there is that new issue of a missing leg.

Perhaps the greatest roadblock to smart smartphone parenting is this simple, unforgiving truth: many adults do not fully appreciate the power of cell phones. For example, would a rational person create a poster with an image of her five year old, write down his or her name, the address where he or she attends school, and affix five thousand copies to the walls of the nearest airport? It sounds bizarre and potentially dangerous, but that would only provide a fraction of the exposure posting that same picture has on Facebook. Yet millions of adults do not think twice about doing just that.

How many politicians, captains of industry, actors, musicians, and others with considerable levels of fame, success, and notoriety have encountered public shaming or suffered a humiliating fall from grace because of their missteps or misdeeds online? Let us not overlook the countless commoners who have silently suffered a similar downfall. All have been intoxicated by the allure of these magical machines and are thereby too impaired to recognize that smartphones harness the potency of Gutenberg's printing press strapped to a fifty-megaton bomb.

In other words, they are not phones.

In fairness, most parents do not have the vantage point of educators and therefore have greater difficulty fathoming how impactful cell phones truly are in the hands of youngsters. The average sample size for parents is only 2.5, while educators observe thousands. Furthermore, for most parents, *What to Expect When You're Expecting* is the first and last book about child rearing they read. This lack of inquisitiveness has both logistical and egotistical roots.

Logistically, after a child is born, parents seldom have time to perpetuate the romance that led to the children in the first place, let alone read up on how technological changes have disrupted the norms of traditional childhood development. Most new learning comes from informal chats with other parents at soccer practice, dinner parties, or in the produce aisle of the neighborhood supermarket. They are lessons of coincidence and convenience more than anything else.

Egotistically, we live in an age in which feeling is believing. Regrettably, individuals seldom go outside of themselves to reflect on what they perceive as truth. When they do, those investigations are quickly satiated by a Google search, sifting through social media posts, or a two-minute YouTube video. While these methods are quite effective when seeking out how to replace your cabin air filter (it is so easy—never pay someone to do it!), it is much more complicated when it involves the social and emotional development of your own children.

Ultimately, parents issue smartphones to their children for two reasons:

1. They succumb to peer pressure—more often than not perpetrated by their own offspring.
2. They enjoy the convenience.
    a. No longer must they knock on the door and make small talk with the playdate mom while junior figures out how to put on his sneakers. Just text "HERE" and remain warm and dry in the car.
    b. No longer must they contemplate waiting five more minutes before calling the police and filing a Missing Child report because junior was supposed to be home in time for dinner but still hasn't arrived.

Amusingly, it is the younger generation often accused of lacking patience and being incapable of accepting delayed satisfaction, when in actuality they are inherited traits. Regrettably, this form of convenience comes at a great expense.

For starters, there is the hardware itself, which can cost anywhere from $400 to $1,000. Tack on another $50 to $100 for accessories, like cases, screen protectors, car chargers, and backup batteries. Then you actually need to provide mobile service for about $30 to $50 each month, per device, depending on the carrier and whether or not there are any overages. (Tweens and teens have a way of eviscerating data plans.) Of course, if something drops, breaks, gets wet, or is damaged, lost, or stolen along the way, these numbers will spike. In the overarching scheme of life, the financial cost is the least significant.

When a parent hands a child $1,000 worth of smartphone gear, he or she immediately becomes a target for theft. (Quizzically, parents also purchase phone wallets for bank and credit cards, as though the device alone wasn't enough of a payday for would-be criminals.) With the cell phone, there is an increased likelihood the child will be distracted when crossing the street, riding a bicycle, walking home, or driving a car. Yet parents comically insist that these devices *increase* safety.

Furthermore, without strict guidelines or an earnest intention to enforce one's prescribed rules when they are inevitably broken, young cell phone recipients immediately find themselves at grave risk of developing an addiction to the device. Pre-adolescents and adolescents are on their phones anywhere between six and nine hours each day. This includes messaging, videos, gaming, etc.

Considering that kids sleep for about seven hours each night and attend school for seven hours each day, that does not leave much nonscreen time. These statistics will soar as more and more school districts incorporate tablets into the classroom. In spite of the potential academic gains, this increase does not bode well for the social and emotional health of children.

More and more stories are surfacing that suggest that doctors across the nation are misdiagnosing children with ADHD, essentially because of cell phones. Throughout the night, young people check, send, and receive group texts, Snapchats, and a bevy of other electronic notifications. Each *bzz-bzz* disrupts normal sleep patterns, which can cause behavioral effects that mirror symptoms for attention and hyperactivity disorders.

Parents are frequently unaware that these fleeting interruptions are even taking place and therefore do not present this critical information to their children's physicians. This misunderstanding can result in youngsters being prescribed medication to treat ailments they do not have.

Writing for *Psychology Today*, Dr. Victoria L. Dunckley explains that the dangers associated with cell phones cross over into the physiological development of the brain. Similar to gaming, using digital devices releases dopamine, which produces a fleeting quasi-high that makes the brain demand more of a given thing, thus increasing the likelihood of addiction. When cell phones are used for an extended period—say, six to nine hours each day—Dunckley notes a number of discernible trends:

1. Atrophy in gray matter areas—young people find it more difficult to suppress the impulses that lead one to engage in socially unacceptable behavior; this negatively impacts the ability to process information and exercise proper judgment.
2. Decreased cortical thickness—frequent use of phones, tablets, and similar gadgets alters the development of the frontal lobe; cognition can be impacted, leading to deficiencies in task performance.

Let's see; an underachieving student with a seemingly low aptitude for making good decisions and a penchant for mistreating his or her peers on social media. Sound like any middle schooler you know? And these physiological changes affecting the brain will not revert back once a device is taken away. This impacts development permanently, which can significantly disrupt socialization.

Peer-to-peer debasement over social media and messaging applications is no small matter. School administrators can fill volumes recounting the horribly abusive ways young people speak to one another. It is not even accurate to refer to it as "speaking" anymore because there is so much more to it. Communication involves the composition of multimodal elements, which add layer upon layer of meaning to the messages. Often adults are unaware of the undertones and connotations hidden in plain sight. Young people are also duping snooping parents by creating aliases and alter egos online. For every Insta, there is likely a Finsta—a thinly veiled version of one's Instagram persona.

It is often in these "anonymous" spaces where the gloves really come off. Educators have previously seen these types of environments with old school applications like Ask FM. In these forums individuals are called out, but typically not by name. This misbehavior often resides at the cyber intersection of therapeutic venting and character assassination. And the taunters are as well disguised as the folks attending the sex party in *Eyes Wide Shut*. These posts often launch a thousand additional posts, providing enough of a tailwind to kick rumor mongering and pot stirring into full effect—as intended.

We do not commonly see these same improprieties in face-to-face interactions. For the most part, young people still extend a modicum of courtesy and respect in traditional environs. However, when they communicate with their thumbs, a Jekyll and Hyde transformation occurs. This lack of civility is not unique to adolescents. Look no further than the trolls of the internet, who populate page after page with personal attacks and venomous rage, often unprovoked. It is as if the rules that govern healthy, normative human interaction cease to exist when two thumbs are placed behind a 5.5-inch screen.

At-risk behaviors, especially involving the young, are also on the rise in the cell phone age. Access to information on drugs, tobacco, and alcohol are at pre-adolescent fingertips. More sinisterly, access to individuals who sell the aforementioned vices are just a text, snap, Voxer, Slack, or WhatsApp away. This is a far cry from the days of dealers and their beepers. Digital tools provide faster, easier, and more universal access to those who wish to profit from the corruption of youth—proffering addiction for cash.

Perhaps nothing epitomizes this premise more than the proliferation of vaping over the past few years. Manufacturers are keying in on teens by designing vapes and e-cigarettes that are simple, small, and sleek, just like the technology with which they are obsessed. The similarity to computer accessories, like flash drives, makes it even easier to conceal these misbehaviors out in the open. Schools are frequently catching students charging their vapes using cell phone backup batteries, purchased by their parents. USB ports know no improprieties.

With flavors like crème brûlée, cool mint, and mango, Big Tobacco 2K19 is successfully breeding a new generation of lifelong nicotine junkies—shrewdly, albeit immorally, leveraging one addiction to fuel another. And these very companies are blessed with millions of dollars of free marketing through the countless selfies that kids post to feature their products.

Furthermore, through YouTube tutorials, young users can quickly learn how to refill their pods or swap out vape juice and replace it with THC oil, a condensed, highly potent, chemical form of marijuana. Making matters worse are the countless shop owners who refuse to abide by age restrictions that were established to protect underage consumers. As a result, whether through modified pods or wax pens—designed specifically for drug consumption—more and more teens are getting sky high in school bathrooms, lockers, and classrooms.

No smell. No sound. No end in sight.

BEYOND HELICOPTERS

There is a growing anxiety that is engulfing modern parenting. The philosophies of prior generations, such as "school of hard knocks" and "what doesn't kill you makes you stronger," have been replaced with "he or she can do no wrong," "one more chance," and "nobody messes with my child." Realistically, the natural challenges that emerge in this world will mess with many a child. Parents seem unwilling or unprepared to allow any setbacks to befall their children from birth until death. This failure to grasp reality is a harbinger for what lies ahead.

For some time, this type of overprotective behavior has been described as "helicopter parenting," but that no longer accurately depicts child rearing in a forward fast world. Helicopters hover from a distance. Parents have determined that observing from above is too impersonal, not quite hands-on enough

To further mollify their apprehension, parents have digitally implanted themselves inside the hip pockets of their children. Finally, they can go back and undo the obstetrician's short-sighted error by virtually reattaching the umbilical cord with smartphone technology. As a result, we are on the cusp of the greatest regression in parenting history since children were removed from schools and placed into factories. Welcome to the age of hip pocket parenting.

The framework of hip pocket parenting centers on a premise called the *reverse kangaroo*. Mama kangaroos carry their young in pouches to keep them protected as they move about. Human mamas (and papas) want teenage children to carry their parents around in pouches, so they can be on hand to make real-time decisions for their offspring. They earnestly believe this will help keep them safe because, as hip pocket parents know, no one can make a better decision for their children than they.

Therefore when children are bequeathed smartphones, they are often required to provide updates of everything, all the time—in class, at lunch, after school, on the way home. It is not uncommon for an administrator to send for a student in class and receive a phone call from an anxiety-ridden parent before the child even makes it down to the main office. Similarly, many dismayed teachers discover that a distracted student is unfocused in class because he or she is engaged in a text exchange with his or her parent. These are the new realities in forward fast schools.

Despite the short-run benefits that its practitioners enjoy, hip pocket parenting has negative long-term implications, primarily because its premise is rooted in fallacy. The most effective way to learn good decision-making skills is by not getting it right the first time. Additionally, young people must be taught to engage in the process of making choices. This begets an understanding that an individual should be willing to forego one thing in exchange for something else one desires.

Last, learning how to live with and work through the repercussions of one's decisions promotes accountability, which is the cornerstone of coping skills—something so many children woefully lack.

Hip pocket parents rob their children of the precious opportunities to develop these critical skills while the stakes are still relatively low. If Malcolm Gladwell's "10,000 Hours" premise applies, young people need to make thousands of decisions before they attain proficiency. If little kids have little problems and big kids have big problems, wouldn't we want them to cut their teeth on the relatively innocuous instead of those choices with tremendous implications?

But hip pocket parents use phones to create roadblocks in the pathway of childhood development. They neither permit children to independently engage in the process nor allow them to take agency and overcome the burdens of getting it wrong, which is infinitely more valuable. This can devolve into a self-fulfilling prophecy. As children demonstrate lousy decision-making abilities, hip pocket parents further insert themselves into the pouch.

During those inevitable instances when life throws young people a curveball, they will likely scapegoat their hip pocket parents, and with good reason. Why would a child accept ownership for a choice he or she did not actually make? This decreased accountability sets the stage for insufficient decision-making skills as children transition into adulthood.

Anyone familiar with *The Godfather* films understands that having someone "in your pocket" implies a certain puppeteer-like control over another individual. This parallel is most befitting, considering how well kids play their parents who are reverse kangarooing. After all, the very roads that built Rome led to its demise.

With a single thumb children can tap directly into the epicenter of their parents' neuroses. My colleagues and I call this manipulative game "Beat the Referral." The first person to weigh in gets to frame the situation however he or she wants. In other words, kids are using smartphones to outsmart their parents.

Look no further than the example of that child who was called down to the administrator's office. While in the stairwell, he is spinning a narrative via messaging that, almost certainly, portrays someone else as the antagonist. It doesn't even matter what the issue is. The average (anxiety-filled) parent immediately raises a number of questions:

1. Why isn't my child comfortable/safe in that school?
2. Who at the school can I blame?
3. Thank God I bought this phone, otherwise how would I be able protect my child?

Perhaps the third item is most disconcerting. The child's manipulation of the phone becomes parental evidence to reinforce the validity of the phone. This is why parents are loath to take their children's phones away. Of course, they claim to, but many often do not because they are addicted to the feeling of having a false sense of security—or, as they put it, "safety."

As anyone who has worked with children can attest, they are not dumb. In fact, for most of our recorded history, exceptional burdens were heaped on the young, ranging from physical labor (farms and factories) to political leadership (kings and queens). It is only in modern times that we have reversed course by lowering expectations and reducing responsibility.

It is also important to note that children very astutely test the fence for weaknesses. They do this incredibly well in the classroom; home is no exception. So when a parent insists that a child include him or her in real-time developments,

- that parent engages in living two lives at once;
- that parent becomes too emotionally invested in the child's socialization because the outcomes were derived by his or her decision making, not the child's (this is a driver of more anxiety); and
- it denies the child the right to successfully navigate life on his or her own. More importantly, it denies him or her the right to fail and learn from it— life's greatest lesson.

Phones may empower, but they can just as easily debilitate. Entering into adulthood with a subpar ability to make choices and cope with outcomes is one of the least safe emotional states a child can find him- or herself in. This calls into question the old refrain: How do phones offer increased safety?

Parents spend considerable sums on sturdy doors, deadbolts, alarm systems, and, more recently, doorbell cameras that can be viewed in real time through an app on one's phone. Yet a ten year old who wishes to belittle your child can appear at your kitchen table in a nanosecond. A sixteen-year-old boy who wishes to show your thirteen-year-old daughter his penis can waltz right past you vegging on the living room couch and into her bedroom without making a sound. And she can easily reciprocate with pornographic images of her own while you toggle through your DVR.

According to research published by *JAMA Pediatrics*, one in seven teens is sexting, while one in four admits to receiving explicit images. This disproportionate ratio of received messages to those sent clues us in on how important sharing is in the social network culture. With the ubiquity of devices— no one needs a class list to contact a peer anymore—and the ease with which images can be transmitted, misdeeds and mistakes travel quickly. And when kids move forward fast, it only takes a split second to memorialize improper judgment.

There is no door, lock, security camera, or automatic assault rifle that can defend one's home against a mediocre Wi-Fi signal.

PARENTAL CONTROLS—A MODERN OXYMORON

In a forward fast world, it is understandable for parents to lack a certain confidence. After all, each preceding generation of parents could recall social or cultural equivalencies that existed in their respective childhoods to serve as touchstones from which to guide or inform motherly or fatherly advice. Then America Online came along and put gunpowder in the keg. Social media poured gasoline all over it. The iPhone lit the match that blew childhood norms to smithereens.

As a result, parents have been left understandably disoriented. It is difficult to keep up with the rate of change. Which apps are good? Which are bad? What is a meme? Who are these four hundred other people who claim to be my child's "friend?" No one knocks on the door and asks if your child can come out to play anymore. No one calls and asks if he or she can speak with your son or daughter anymore. No child gets to come home at the end of a rotten day, close his or her door, flop down on his or her bed, and know that the day is over anymore. The horrors of the day live on into the night. Before anything dies, the hoards must have their say. This is not good.

Lousy days are a child's rite of passage. They always have been. What is new and incredibly damaging to the emotional development of the young is the permanence of life in a fishbowl. The mantra "kids will be kids" can no longer be used to explain away bad deeds because children have the means to magnify anger, expose flaws, and prey on weakness in ways never before imagined. Circumstances are no longer the same, so old sayings no longer apply.

As these devices and their related applications become more and more powerful, parents are losing more and more control. On one hand, there is a technological gap that exists for many. While young people do not always understand the finer points of how networks and servers interact to make the web a reality, they are quick studies when it comes to misdirection and hiding inappropriate content on their phones.

Many parents are unaware of the tools offered by their carriers to exercise greater control over their children's devices. More embarrassingly, a large number of parents allow their kids to place passwords on devices, essentially locking out the person who pays for the technology. Imagine coming home to find the locksmith changing the tumbler on the front door, then handing the only key to your fourteen-year-old son.

Generational gaps in technological prowess are to be expected. The less forgivable cause of childhood cell phone abuse is that many kids are learning horrible digital habits from their parents. They observe how adults are the perpetrators and producers of low brow, infantile consumption. Kids yearn for the opportunity to have devices of their own, so they can play their version of grown-up games. So in many households the blind are leading the blind.

Our thumbs have gotten us pretty far in this world. It would be a shame if we allowed them to become the bane of our existence. But right now, the internet is a lot like the Wild West.

It is time for the sheriff to roll into town and lay down the law.

Chapter Six

From P.E. to I.E.

Northampton, Massachusetts, 1823

Leaders from the Round Hill School conduct a meeting in which they reimagine the daily school experience for their students and, unknowingly, alter the way millions of children will be educated over the better part of the next two centuries. This seemingly innocuous curriculum change will prove to be a small step for children but a giant step for childrenkind. What decision did these educational leaders make that was so impactful?

The Round Hill School required young people to participate in physical education.

Of course, incorporating athletics into a wide array of academic subjects was hardly a new idea. The Greeks touted the importance of a "sound mind and sound body" more than two thousand years earlier. (Which should remind us that great ideas need not be new ideas. Ours is to uncover ways to synthesize the old with the new and establish relevance in the present.) Nearly fifty years into our nation's development, life was changing for the people of Northampton and elsewhere.

Less than one hundred miles away, in Lowell, American industrialization was taking a massive leap forward with the establishment of a textile mill, the likes of which no one had ever seen. The ripple effect of these changes bred unfamiliar societal transformations. These transformations took a social and emotional toll on children whose family lives were disrupted by technological innovations.

When developments move forward fast, it is easy to lose perspective. The educators at the Round Hill School wisely sought to mitigate these profound changes by deviating from past practice. They weren't simply looking to teach the same old curriculum in new ways, they desired to do something new within the established framework of the schoolhouse. As we rapidly progress through our own modern technological revolution, we could learn a thing or two from our predecessors hailing from New England. (As a New York Giants fan, it's difficult to give props to anything from Tom Brady country, but fair is fair.)

The sale of WhatsApp is a stark reminder of how new technologies can impact markets and the workforces that sustain them. In 2014, Facebook purchased the popular messaging app for $19 billion. At that time, the company only had fifty-five employees. Based on that price, each employee was generating roughly $350 million of value. If the Ford Motor Company's two hundred thousand employees created that kind of productivity, it would be worth $70 trillion! Yet the market capitalization of Ford is *only* $44 billion.

With that in mind, today's educational leaders and school boards need to beware the emerging "Tulip-mania" of engineering and technology-related degrees. As more and more courses are offered in coding, engineering, app design, and the like, two potential problems emerge. First, while these curricula offer students the opportunity to develop specific skills that are among the cornerstones of our Information Age economy, they will not necessarily be of value to *all* or even most students.

Second, when the market becomes flooded with developers and systems experts, the salaries they command will likely plummet—even though the cost of earning their degrees will undoubtedly rise. This may very well trigger a modern reboot of the Farmers' Alliance, this time with engineers at the epicenter.

Despite chatter about the supposed proliferation of computer engineering and coding jobs, the majority of young people who pass through our hallways will be consumers, not producers, of technological tools. They will proficiently drag, drop, swipe, and click using applications and hardware designed by others to generate their own content and complete necessary tasks, but few will require more than a basic level of knowledge.

Therefore we must try to keep our perspective before we hop on too many bandwagons. Schools were not solely derived with the intention of providing children with vocational knowledge. If they were, each student would spend most of his or her day mastering the principles of plumbing and electricity, which are practically ignored in our curricula yet are the backbone of our modernized existence.

Better yet, why not teach everyone how to run fiber optic cable or set up Wi-Fi drops? We are depicting an idyllic future in the literal and figurative clouds while ignoring the magic beanstalk required to get kids there.

Of course, there is no reason to ban technology-related courses either. We simply must determine the best way to distribute our precious and sometimes diminishing resources. School budgets have been exceptionally tight in recent years. These economic conditions come from a combination of wasteful spending, an exploding population of special needs students, and a seemingly new mentality that many have acquired in which they demand more from their public institutions but strenuously resist paying for the additional services they crave. It's a bizarre, twenty-first-century American corollary to Marxism—from each, nothing more; to each, everything he desires.

This philosophical fallacy flies in the face of the generations that preceded us. Those folks came together to do big things, whether it was the creation of great cities, building infrastructure to move people and goods to and from, turning back the forces of fascism, Nazism, communism, and imperialism, or laying the foundation of a well-educated populous through a network of beautifully constructed public schools.

These were not happy accidents. They were intentional acts, with one eye on the present and an even keener eye on the future. They were acts of passion, selflessness, and love. Most elementary school classroom door knobs in New York City's public schools were made of brass and engraved with the name of the school. Many, if not all, have since been stolen and replaced with the cheapest substitutes on the district bid list. That says so much about where we've been and how far we have come.

This brings us back to Northampton. With change in the air and pressure to transform public schools into incubators of factory-ready adults, school leaders took measures ensuring that young people were not merely being prepared for factory life but rather were ready for life in a world with factories. There is a tremendous difference.

Taking time each day to address a child's physical and emotional needs became the foundation upon which P.E. was born. It transcended the simple notion of play—recess, without structure or content, could meet those basic needs. P.E. was designed to be play with a purpose.

Over time, P.E. became a requirement, expanding to include the introduction of cultural elements such as dance and music. Through participation, students learned lessons of teamwork, winning, losing, friendly competition, and sustaining a healthier mindset over the course of one's life.

Today, if we simply create courses that teach computer- and web-based skills, students will only learn how to complete tasks involving the internet rather than understand how to thrive in a world with an internet. Therefore, we need I.E. (Internet Ethics) every bit as much as Northampton needed P.E. (Physical Education) 150 years ago.

WHY I.E.?

We can agree that the internet is not a passing fad. Arguably, it is responsible for the most profound disruption to human life, on a global level, in recorded history. Short of knocking the planet off its axis, new technologies have rocked the world to its core. It has permanently altered how we shop, travel, communicate, exchange money, receive health care, consume entertainment, find love, elect leaders, revolt against them, learn new tasks, and teach young people who have never experienced life any other way.

Yet despite all of the brilliance and majesty bestowed upon us by our new devices, we are witnessing the emergence of a new normal in schools: children behaving badly. Very badly.

Young people are clearly having major difficulties navigating life in a tech-laden world. A proverb in Ecclesiasticus perhaps helps us shed some light on why: *You have been shown more than you can understand.*

Ain't that the truth??

To be fair, we have moved forward so fast that adults have hardly come to understand the true power of what we hold in our hands. It's definitely cool, but at what cost? To a significant degree, it has also disrupted the good and set fire to social norms. The empowerment offered by new technology is leaving many pre-adolescents and adolescents to explore the depths of moral corruption on a scale never before seen. They congregate in virtual spaces, far from adult eyes, and treat one another in the most vile, disrespectful ways, marrying abusive language, insensitive epithets, and demoralizing visuals. This is far beyond "kids being kids." They too have been shown way more than they can possibly understand.

So what are we to do?

Well, the first part of the aforementioned proverb suggests: *Do not meddle in matters that are beyond you.* At the risk of committing blasphemy, this is exactly the wrong course of action when it comes to technology. As educators, we are compelled to meddle; it is our moral and professional imperative.

When you really break it down, our society only has two institutions charged with teaching, imparting, and upholding our nation's ethical and philosophical values: schools and courts. If education doesn't win the day, incarceration likely awaits. Therefore it is imperative that we meddle. Implementing a vibrant I.E. curriculum in schools will help us all gain a better understanding of what we have been shown and allow us to construct a plan to move into the future with clarity, free of compunction.

In other words, we need I.E.

WHAT DOES I.E. LOOK LIKE?

In order to maximize the impact of this type of curriculum, instruction needs to begin at the elementary level. We have all been to restaurants and watched toddlers, who can't walk or talk, yet they are operating a smart device from the high chair or mom's lap. If children are going to start early, so must we. What follows are a few samples of what may comprise thought-provoking, rigorous I.E. courses.

Elementary Level

Big Idea: The internet is a wonderful, amazing tool that allows people from all over the world to come together, share ideas, exchange information (content), become more informed individuals, and contribute to the common good. It also challenges us to conduct ourselves in such a way as to respect the rights and freedoms of others while sharing a virtual space.

Lesson

Aim: Should the wireless telegraph be considered the "first internet?"
Students will:

1. identify Samuel Morse, Morse Code, telegraph, and technological disruption;
2. explain how the wireless telegraph worked;
3. compose a message/Tweet/Snap using Morse Code;
4. evaluate the positive and negative ways the wireless telegraph "disrupted" life in the mid-1800s;
5. explain how the internet works and the extent to which it "disrupts" life today;
6. compare/contrast the differences between the two; and
7. assess the extent to which the wireless telegraph can be considered "the first internet."

Lesson

Aim: Should electronic communication have rules?
Students will:

1. identify ham radio, CB, protocol, and electronic communication;
2. explain the evolution in wireless communication from the telegraph to ham radio to CB to the internet (understanding the basic science behind each);
3. analyze the protocols of communication through ham radio and CB;
4. conduct a conversation using these rules;
5. discuss the benefits and burdens of utilizing those protocols;
6. evaluate the differences between face-to-face communication and electronic communication; and
7. debate whether or not rules could/should be established to regulate the internet.

Lesson

Aim: How can we respond when people behave inappropriately toward us online?

Students will:

1. identify inappropriate language, tone, piling on, ganging up, and bullying;
2. explain whether or not students prefer to communicate with friends via digital messaging or through actual face-to-face conversation;
3. analyze how common words, such as "thanks," can be read with different tones by the recipient of a message;
4. assess ways to clear up possible misinterpretations of tone through their written communications (for example, how you use ellipses, emojis, punctuation);
5. evaluate different approaches to handling situations in which one feels mistreated or belittled on the internet; and
6. rate which approach is most powerful (and realistic).

It may sound a bit bizarre, but in this unprecedented age of information and communication, people are ostensibly less effective in conveying thoughts to one another. It's definitely not from a lack of sharing, but it is less like communication and more like faux-munication—full of sound and fury but signifying nothing. (Yet another example of Shakespeare's prescience.) Apparently we're moving too quickly to fully realize how little we are truly saying to one another anymore. Students are hardly an exception.

Look no further than the average student's ability to sustain a cohesive argument for any significant period of time, whether verbally or in writing. You would struggle mightily as well if you hardly exercised those cognitive muscles on a regular basis. It's faster and simpler to "LOL" or "TY" your way through the day. For some, typing abbreviations is seemingly too taxing, resulting in a stream of thumbs ups or handshakes. Socrates must be ROIHG.

There are also many health implications that derive from excessive amounts of screen time. Nearly every study measuring the levels of childhood activity indicates steady declines over the past ten years. Jerry Seinfeld once joked that when he was a kid he could take one sip from the rusty water fountain and run around all day.

Today, young people claim to need Red Bull, Starbucks, and iced tea in cans as long as their arms in order to sit down and play a videogame. This type of stagnation is likely a harbinger of skyrocketing rates of obesity and heart disease in the future.

The concept of ethics challenges us to explore our actions—put them on trial, if you will. As most good twelve-step programs will suggest, the first meaningful attempt to move forward involves coming to terms with the reality that you have a problem. Many young people are unaware there is even a discussion to be had. It is therefore the prerogative of schools to force the issue.

Once I.E. is taught, it can be incorporated into a school's culture. More than just coursework, these precepts should fuel student expectations. They are digital dharma. They allow all teachers, administrators, counselors, and students to speak in one common language. Through consistency of message, we will inspire productive change.

It's time for I.E. In fact, we're way overdue.

Chapter Seven

The Ten Truths about Tech

Approximately two decades after the first desktop computers popped up in classrooms and departmental offices, many teachers and administrators have come to the realization that this is not a wave of technology but rather a tsunami. Disaster movies completely misrepresent the impact of tsunamis as the first large swell isn't the most impactful, it just lets you know change is underway.

The real shock is felt when the force of the incoming water continues to exert pressure everywhere and on everything. That unstoppable, steady stream lifts objects from their moorings and pushes them to places never before conceived. Some go with the flow, while others cling for dear life onto whatever tree branch they can reach. Either way, almost nothing and no one is left unaffected.

While our transition into this new way of living, learning, and interacting has introduced us all to a wealth of new tools and a bevy of fresh opportunities, there are certain truths about tech that are worth examining.

NUMBER 10: TECH IS SUPPOSED TO SAVE US TIME, BUT IT DOESN'T (AKA TECHPOCRISY).

Ironically, as the processing speeds of computing devices get faster and faster, the amount of time teachers and administrators spend completing tasks using these supposedly speedier tools gets longer and longer. The very technology that promised to be the ultimate modern convenience has inadvertently stolen copious amounts of our most valuable resource, as if the microwave is slower than the oven.

Educators feel this techpocrisy on a daily basis. Consider these old-world practices:

- Assign homework by writing it on the chalkboard. Done.
- Notify parents of everything with a "Welcome Back" letter. Done.
- Distribute report cards to students four times a year to share academic progress. Done.
- Check mailboxes in the morning (aka once a week, or for some annually) to get information. Done.

Thanks to techpocrisy, educators are now never truly done. Ever. It's not as though teachers and administrators have replaced any of these traditional responsibilities with new tasks. We have only *added to them*. To further the problem, the more we all do, the more others expect. The similar list of professional responsibilities now looks something like this:

- Check mailbox *and* email *and* shared drive folders.
- Write the "Welcome Back" letter *and* quarterly updates *and* monthly reminders *and* post each week's activities on the school website.
- Distribute four report cards *and* four progress reports *and* maintain up-to-the-minute grades in a published electronic gradebook, which is reviewable in real time throughout the entire school year. (Oh, and be prepared to field calls and emails regarding those grades as they are posted.)
- Place homework on the whiteboard *and* on your website *and* in your shared drive *and* send reminder messages to students telling them about the homework in case they missed the other three locations.

Unlike the rosy image of convenience and simplicity promised by *The Jetsons*, in a techpochrisy, the faster machines go, the faster people are expected to move in order to keep pace with them. *More* no longer comes by way of addition but rather is exponential. Perhaps George Jetson said it best: "Jane, stop this crazy thing!"

NUMBER 9: TECH INCREASES SCRUTINY, DESERVED OR NOT.

Educators have always been (very) minor celebrities within their respective communities. How many trips to the mall or a restaurant have unexpectedly turned into teacher sightings? It's not quite Biebermania, but it will give you slight pause when you are about to head out for your Saturday jaunt in *those* jeans. Occasionally, students run in the opposite direction, but more often than not, parents and kids saunter over and chat for a minute (or sporadically conduct an unscheduled parent-teacher conference—this is particularly undesirable on the beach or at Disney World!).

While one may occasionally receive the benefit of an extra scoop of ice cream or a table with a nicer view because a former student works at the particular establishment one enjoys frequenting, the drawbacks of living in a fishbowl of any size are significant. Whether they are being praised on the bleachers or blasted in the produce aisle, educators are talked about. Technology exacerbates this chatter in two unfortunate ways.

First, lay people have more access to a teacher's materials than ever. This would not be a big deal were it not for the reality that they are often examined out of context. Once parents start clicking, they often refuse to stop until they find another teacher who has the "right amount" or better materials online. Then the unfair comparisons begin.

Absent is an understanding of methodology, intention, or a true sense of what complementary pieces are utilized within the classroom walls. (Of course, there is the possibility that a teacher is doing a less than stellar job and that is clearly reflected in his or her digital footprint.)

Second, when certain aforementioned individuals determine that a given teacher has not met their interpretation of muster, they take to the web to castigate him or her. Look no further than your local community's Facebook page to find the latest flogging. Perhaps this forum was originally intended to share recipes or get a new stoplight at that busy intersection in town, but then again, Adam and Eve were supposed to grow old in the Garden of Eden.

This deleterious side effect of the internet has wormed its way into nearly all facets of the community. Derogatory comments about restaurants, hotels, politicians, movies, and a host of other topics abound. Frankly, most remarks are embarrassing and an utter waste of bandwidth. There is something particularly unseemly about parents who behave as trolls and direct animus toward the individuals who educate their children, especially given how much access they have to the school and its faculty.

To be fair, teachers and administrators are far from perfect and should be held to the highest standards. Therefore parents and community members have the right to express reasonable concerns regarding their children or neighborhood school, utilizing the proper channels. However, it is in very poor taste to utilize the court of public opinion to disparage or discredit those who have dedicated their professional lives to serving the educational, social, and emotional needs of their very own flesh and blood.

NUMBER 8: MOST YOUNG PEOPLE STINK AT TECH.

Considering that almost every kid has been pinching or swiping some form of touchscreen since he or she developed fine motor skills and has been literally awash in technology since being scanned in the womb, children have an incredibly limited understanding of how any of it works. Don't be fooled by how proficiently they toggle through their phones or tablets: most young people stink at tech. If you don't believe this, hide the ethernet cable that connects the modem to the router and see how quickly your Wi-Fi gets back up and running.

Of course, a handful of students are incredibly knowledgeable. Administrators know them as the ones who have figured out how to circumvent the school's firewall to play *Fortnight* on their district-issued devices or hack into the learning management system to access schedules and grades. But these truly clever kids are few and far in between.

The parents of Generation Z lived through the transition and experienced the growing pains. They can differentiate between an ethernet cable and a phone cord. They recognize floppy disks, red, white, and yellow RCA plugs, and remember the distinct shrill of dial-up. They struggled to comprehend user manuals, spent hours on the phone getting tech support, and lugged hardware to and from repair centers in the hopes of getting the darn machine to work because the premise of replacing appliances as the first and only act of troubleshooting was not yet part of the cultural ethos.

Millennials and Gen Xers did not grow up with this latest incarnation of touchscreen technology but rather grew through it. As a result, they have accrued many insights over that time. Among them is the understanding that with each passing generation there is less and less of an interest in logistics or how these magical things do what they do. Nearly a century ago, when a Depression-era teen, like my grandfather, wanted to listen to the radio, he or she often went to the hardware store, bought a transistor and a few other cheap parts, locked him- or herself in the garage, and didn't surface until he or she could hear the latest episode of *Captain Midnight*.

This high level of inquisitiveness and improvisation—coupled with Depression-driven necessity—has been replaced by a growing expectation that one should have everything and that it must always work. This culture has been ingrained through the production of technological goods that are designed for obsolescence, yielding a never-ending cycle of consumerism. (Automobile companies have satiated this same desire through the proliferation of leasing cars.)

There was a time when companies would brag about how well their products were made and how *in*frequently they needed to be replaced. Consumers would properly maintain or repair their possessions to prolong their usefulness. In a forward fast world, everything exists in beta, intimating that everything is fleeting; the only constant is change.

The result is a new generation that has little inclination to invest time discovering the hows and whys of new tech, unless it's something relatively superficial, like a photo filter or multigesture shortcut. As a result, the young have a limited sense of where all of this change falls along the continuum of innovation. Lack of context begets a lack of appreciation. It is difficult to magnify the value of technology as a learning tool with such a dearth of understanding.

NUMBER 7: SOMETIMES TECH IS NOT THE ANSWER.

As schools move forward fast and classrooms ramp up the installation of Wi-Fi drops, presentation equipment, and access to endless apps, it is important to remember that sometimes technology is *not* the answer. This is a painful realization for some educational leaders to hear, especially those who staked their reputation by convincing school Boards to drop huge dollar amounts acquiring all of these expensive new toys. But educators cannot serve two masters.

It is easy for bias or the politicization of school hierarchies to have an undue influence on a teacher's methodology and practice. Technology companies do not help matters as they attest that their products are the only way to properly teach in the twenty-first century. Therefore it is not uncommon for educators to feel a certain pressure, citing, "I have to use it because *they* want me to." When people begin using technology simply for its own sake, it detracts from methodological intentionality, which undermines quality instruction.

In a perfect world, teachers have theoretical and experiential reasons to support the actions they take and the lessons they design. If one is going to maintain these standards, it is reasonable to expect that, from time to time, it will be concluded that technology is not the answer.

Quite simply, it is okay to occasionally put the *no* in technology. As former chairman of the People's Republic of China Deng Xiaoping once said, "It doesn't matter if the cat is black or white, as long as it catches mice." All educators would be wise to keep their collective eyes on the ball and recognize that technology is a means to an end and not the end itself.

NUMBER 6: TECH LEVELS THE PLAYING FIELD WHILE SIMULTANEOUSLY EXACERBATING OUR DIFFERENCES.

Like sneakers and hoodies, technology can influence social status among young people. Imagine being the kid who takes out an iPhone 5 at a lunch table full of XSs, or worse, has no phone at all. It is as bad as sporting Asics kicks in a schoolyard filled with the latest LeBrons. School districts try to counter this disparity by providing devices on a 1:1 basis, but not all are able to afford these types of technological initiatives. This heightens the disparities between neighborhoods and the children living in them.

Of course, the limited availability of technology seems like the least of the socioeconomic deficiencies when one considers the dangers of poverty, inadequate access to nutritious foods, insufficient health care, high crime rates, and a dearth of affordable, safe housing. These exigencies can be found in urban and rural settings alike. No one group of people owns hardship and struggle.

However, if school leaders anticipate that arming students and teachers with tablets or computers will promote higher levels of learning and increased cognitive abilities, then they are setting the haves and have nots on two completely different academic paths to the future. If there are concerns about the achievement gap now, imagine what the future might look like.

It is therefore imperative that there is support of any and all measures to provide access to as many disparate communities as possible, both domestically and internationally. A rising technological tide will lift all learners and open the throttle, allowing our collective societies to enjoy the benefits of interconnectivity and the totality of humankind's potential.

NUMBER 5: TECH WILL FAIL YOU, OFTEN WHEN YOU NEED IT MOST.

If Murphy, whom the hard luck law was named after, lived in the modern age, he most definitely would have included technology as the centerpiece of his code.

The classroom SMART Board worked perfectly periods one and two, but when your supervisor enters during period three, it freezes up.

When you are making a presentation to every parent in the community, the video won't play, or it will buffer for minutes at a time. (Note: These minutes will feel like decades.)

The lesson you spent hours crafting and tweaking until it was perfect will disappear from your drive inexplicably (most likely when that same supervisor shows up). Any attempts to explain it away will harken back to the time the dog ate your homework, yet this phenomenon is real.

Considering that technology is constructed from inanimate objects that are designed, actualized, installed, and maintained by humans, it has the same unpredictability and temperament as its flesh-and-blood creators. This has only been the cautionary tale of every single work of science fiction ever created; however, when this happens it inexplicably takes us by surprise.

It is this predictable unpredictability upon which many technophobes desperately rely. It's the last vestige of hope to support their worldview that the only way to do something is the way we have always done it. When you are stuck in those moments of technological failure, it is very easy to find solace in what they are preaching.

NUMBER 4: DIGITIZATION BREEDS JEALOUSY, ANGER, AND DEPRESSION.

There is an old adage, "What you don't know can't hurt you," which sounds nice but is complete nonsense. Medieval townspeople didn't know about germ theory and more than one-third perished from the Black Plague. That had to hurt. Yet despite the gaps in logic, we tend to share this advice with young people so they do not harp on what they are unaware of or cannot understand. And for a few thousand years that worked fairly well.

However, thanks to technology—most notably the toxic marriage of digital cameras and social media—there is hardly anything you don't know; everyone knows everything as it is happening. Mind you, the moments being captured and shared are not run-of-the-mill happenings, they are the extremes—at least that is how they are framed.

BEST PARTY EVER
WORST DAY OF MY LIFE
FUNNIEST VIDEO ROFL
BIGGEST LOSER

When was the last time you saw a post that read "HAD A FAIRLY NICE TIME"? Isn't it possible that something we do is just *meh* or *so-so*? Or maybe something was boring. Must it be SOOOOO BORING!!!? Perhaps our collective desire to use superlatives is derived from an insecure subconscious trying to turn the mundane into the extraordinary, justifying that our existence is shareable. Or more pointedly, when exposed to an endless stream of images depicting others living out loud, people feel an urgency to validate that they are also enjoying a full life.

Trying to keep up with this digitally fabricated rat race can have a crippling emotional impact on children. Developmentally, many are incapable of recognizing that most people's lives are not as exciting or jam packed with exceptional moments as they appear online. Yet this is their perception of reality. It is reinforced everywhere they look: television, YouTube, social media.

Often the only place where life does not appear enthralling or special is in their own homes, but boring doesn't get Likes. This can inspire adolescents to engage in activities that are post-worthy (selfies of smoking, drug use, sex, etc.) or become the antecedent for jealousy, anger, or depression.

* The final three are grouped together because they comprise the holy trinity of technological truths:

NUMBER 3: THERE IS NO PRIVACY ON THE INTERNET; NUMBER 2: THERE IS NO SECURITY ON THE INTERNET; NUMBER 1: THE INTERNET NEVER FORGETS.

In the totality of human experience, spanning time and space, we have never come up against something possessing the magnitude and permanence of SEND. The polar opposite of Keats, in a forward fast world our names are writ in indelible ink. Every message that is shared, every photo that is taken, every trinket that is purchased, every search that is sought can be—and likely is—recorded . . . forever.

Like infinity, space, and God, SEND is virtually unfathomable. The failure of adults to grasp the potency of this concept is made even direr by their inability to convey its significance to children.

While technology companies may spend billions ensuring their own security, they have yet to adequately acknowledge—or even be held accountable for—how they endanger the well-being of their users, especially the young. *User* is such a perfect word too. We are not *customers* because we are the product.

Millions naively believe that adjusting the privacy settings actually means something. However, that tab, along with the absurdly lengthy and fine print–laden terms of service, really exists to indemnify the creator of the technology. Once lulled into a false sense of equilibrium, users have incredulously demonstrated a willingness to click SEND, no matter what the content.

The result has been an unparalleled, decade-long data dump in which people have uploaded everything from bank account numbers to nude photographs. This has set the stage for an equally unparalleled series of breaches: Equifax, Target, Sony, Wells Fargo, eBay, Yahoo, JP Morgan Chase, WikiLeaks, Uber, Home Depot, and Anthem. Then there are the notoriously self-inflicted wounds: Anthony Weiner, the dentist who killed Cecil the Lion, Gilbert Gottfried, white supremacists taking selfies while white supremacing at Charlottesville, etc.

Of course, for every SEND there is a RECEIVE. This has literally left our treasured democracy susceptible to hacks, transgressions, and dangerous levels of misinformation.

All of this has occurred while our society is still in digital diapers. For the well-being of our children, we must make clear the potential perils of the Information Age.

With SEND there are no redos, retractions, or redacting. With SEND we irrevocably surrender any expectations of privacy or sequestration. With SEND we subject ourselves to unparalleled scrutiny from which we can never escape. There is no more Great Beyond. No heaven. No hell. We all spend eternity in Prineville, Oregon, Loudoun County, Virginia, Pryor Creek, Oklahoma, and wherever else Facebook, Amazon, and Google build their server farms.

And that's the triple truth, Ruth.

Chapter Eight

Pumped Up Kicks

When it comes to changing the game in schools, technology has not been the only show in town over the past twenty years. Regrettably, another force has been unleashed that has propelled everyone fearfully forward just as fast. At 11:19 a.m. on April 20, 1999, students, teachers, and parents in every school building and community tacitly transgressed into an era of anxiety, instability, and darkness. This was the dawn of the age of the school massacre.

For the five or six decades prior to Harris and Klebold maliciously entering Columbine High School donning trench coats and an arsenal, school safety protocols—like classroom technology—remained relatively stagnant. Each year, teachers ushered their children through an anthology of formalities and, depending on the state of détente, an air raid drill or two. These were rote preparations for essentially faceless dangers whose likelihood seemed rather random and unlikely. Now, however, we can name the evils. Even scarier are the names we have yet to know.

Because incidents of school violence have escalated so swiftly and tragically, communities have understandably been called on to do more in the name of safety and protection. New cottage industries have emerged with the latest solutions incorporating technology ranging from bulletproof safe rooms to bowls of stones to be thrown at a classroom intruder. Yes, we are reviving Old Testament tools to disarm machine gun–laden Philistines. Anything to slow down an active shooter and lower the death count until the armored trucks arrive with soldiers bearing heavy artillery. So goes our new mindset.

All of these improved safety measures come with price tags. New doors, locks, cameras, windows, security equipment, metal detectors, and firearm training do not come cheap. Will these expenditures replace funds that otherwise would have been earmarked for books, technology, and teacher training? Or will new money materialize through things like grants and other funding opportunities?

Will schools in wealthier communities be safer because they can afford to be? This would further compromise the immoral and woefully unacceptable gaps that exist among races, classes, ethnicities, and the like.

The age of the school massacre comes with costs that go well beyond money. No longer will children be bestowed with the blessing of naiveté. Brooding, insecurity, and paranoia have infiltrated popular music. The Foster the People song "Pumped Up Kicks," with imagery invoking school shootings, spent weeks on the charts.

Many bopped along as it played on the radio without knowing the deeper message in its lyrics until much later on, or ever. The song essentially suggests that school kids lace up their sneakers so they can outrun impending bullets—not quite the good old days when the music teens listened to only propagated sex, alcohol, and drug use.

UNWANTED KICKS

From early ages children are introduced into our newfound customs and practices. Shoes off at the airport. Security wand at the ball game. Cowering in corners of classrooms while school administrators and police officers rattle door knobs, trying to identify potential vulnerabilities. These little ones do not need to hear the phrases *terrorism*, *lockdown*, and *active shooter* to know that something is terribly awry.

While making a presentation to educators on Long Island, New York, a law enforcement officer shared the story of an elementary-age girl who surprised her parents by returning the Christmas present she had recently received. The parents could not understand why their daughter, who had begged them for months, no longer wanted to wear her new sneakers.

When pressed for a reason, the little girl confessed that she was afraid her shoes would light up while she was hiding from a school shooter. This is indicative of the emotional toll these acts of violence are taking. And it is not only affecting kids.

PERCEPTION VERSUS REALITY

Shortly after the tragedy at Marjory Stoneman Douglas High School in Parkland, Florida, a parent called and engaged me in a rather uncomfortable conversation. He demanded to know how school administrators like myself are going to *guarantee* his child's safety. In a moment that surely pleased the ghost of Socrates but clearly not this parent, this question was answered with another question.

How do *you* guarantee your child's safety?

See, *guarantee* is an interesting word. With the exception of death, there are no guarantees in this world. (Thanks to the miracle of modern corporate accounting, Ben Franklin's maxim about death and taxes now has one assurance too many.) The fact of the matter is that schools could never guarantee safety any more than the Department of Homeland Security could keep Americans safe from terrorist attacks using a color-coded chart. Schools cannot even guarantee that every child will be effectively educated, and the system is built to accomplish that very task.

We need to recalibrate our language.

Perhaps what that parent meant to ask was, "How are you going to make me feel better about sending my child to school?" To answer that question one can enumerate the myriad new safety procedures, security upgrades, and personnel training. However, the sad truth is that we could spend millions of dollars—money we do not have—to build ten-foot-thick steel walls around our grounds and put snipers on the roof, along with an Apache helicopter hovering in the sky above, yet at 3 o'clock we would still need to open the gates to let our students go home. At that moment, anyone armed with a minivan could wreak havoc and take lives if so inclined.

If we look deeper at this parent's original question, it actually speaks to a number of larger issues involving how technology has changed the way we think and behave— in short, our first-world expectations. Thanks to smartphones and web-enabled tablets, society has evolved philosophically to the point at which we now believe that we control anything we wish.

This transformation started generations ago when we first slapped on wristwatches and became much more conscious of time. When we moved to digital, we stopped rounding time because that was inefficient. It's simple math: if we can increase the number of minutes available to us, we can reduce the number of choices we must make, thereby diminishing the need to make sacrifices. In other words, we can now have more of what we want, supposedly maximizing our happiness. More yes; less no. Of course, in actuality, we are typically not happier, just busier. This ushered in a new phenomenon titled "How am I supposed to get it all done?"

Technology turbocharged the time maximization mantra while simultaneously attempting to resolve the "get it done" problem with the help of endless apps, allowing us to talk, text, make restaurant reservations, complete the check-in for tomorrow's flight, and order granola bars while streaming Beyoncé's latest track.

That used to take an entire afternoon. Now we can complete this litany of to-dos standing on line at Starbucks (unless you order ahead with their app, in which case you would handle all of this business in your car, at a red light, while drinking your latte). We have each, in our own way, become what Tom Wolfe once coined "Masters of the Universe."

More specifically, we have not become masters of *the* universe, but rather, masters of *our* universe—individualized and delivered to us in real time. We never miss a television show, phone call, post, article, exit on the highway, or anything anymore unless we choose to miss it. In a weird way, technology has made us godlike. Omnipresent. Powerful. So when gunshots ring out in a high school a thousand miles away, we demand safety in the havens we've created for ourselves.

This puts leaders in a quandary. How do you gingerly remind someone with a god complex that he or she is not a god? Doing so risks confronting a godlike wrath, which is why so many elect to create the perception of safety, knowing full well that it is no longer, nor has it ever been, a reality.

SEEKING AN ANSWER

Of course, it is not good enough to reach a level of existential acceptance when it comes to violence in schools. Our nation's most precious resources fill these cafeterias, libraries, auditoriums, and classrooms. Therefore we have a moral imperative to uncover ways to make our buildings as safe as we can while still preserving the openness and accessibility that encompass the joys of living in a democratic society.

Establishing some version of martial law is not the right direction for the simple reason that schools opting for that environment won't really be any safer, just scarier. At the end of the day, a building is only as secure as the knucklehead student who pops open a locked exit for a stranger or a friend, then continues on to class, or a lazy adult who wedges a stapler in the door jamb so he or she won't need to walk around when he or she returns from the local deli. There are a million versions of these frailties—daily momentary lapses in judgment that typically do not come back to haunt us. Typically.

We can collectively spend fortunes transforming our schools into heavily fortified fortresses, but the next massacre will inevitably be something completely different. It will circumvent and render useless every new safety measure put in place. It is being dreamed up right now by a very clever, very resourceful, very angry young person seated in a classroom in a yet-to-be-named school.

This young person will likely not be stopped by purchase orders, town halls meetings, student walkouts, or even an armed security aide. He or she (statistically speaking, he) will not be swayed by empty campaign slogans, public service announcements, or moments of silence. These methods are far too impersonal. They call attention to the problems of the collective but not the problems of the individual.

Yet, there is a way forward fast. There is hope for a solution. But will we have the temerity to get up close and personal to do what needs to be done?

Chapter Nine

A Paucity of PPS

Despite what the screaming heads on cable news claim, there are common sense measures we could take to make firearms less available to young people without heading down a slippery slope that ends with the decimation of the Second Amendment. But good luck making that argument in this political environment. Truth be told, school massacres are not, at heart, a gun issue any more than my sweet tooth is a Kit Kat issue. It runs much deeper.

The people who brought us "curriculum and testing" to solve every academic issue now want us to believe that "guns and doors" will solve school violence. They won't for the simple reason that these acts of vitriol are a people issue, therefore it will take an army of well-trained people to stem the tide.

To make real progress, please consider the following formula: for every dollar schools spend on security upgrades to prevent shootings, they should spend ten dollars expanding the pupil personnel department, bringing in more counselors and clinicians.

Of course, many districts and state treasuries will immediately point to revenue shortfalls and a laundry list of other programs competing for limited resources. Yet when tragedy regrettably strikes, money somehow materializes to bring in grief counselors after the evil has been perpetrated. And when the unthinkable occurs, like it did at Sandy Hook Elementary, a brand new building was erected to replace the haunted halls where the nightmare took place. This cost the taxpayers of Connecticut $50 million, previously unbudgeted.

And twenty-six souls.

In the age of the school massacre, you either pay up front or you pay dearly at the end. Though the odds indicate that most schools will be free of violence, the technological tools that have shrunk the world assure us that when any school suffers, the sadness, despair, acrimony, and cries for help will reverberate in classrooms and faculty lounges everywhere.

A SAWBUCK FOR A SINGLE

For those who may balk at this ratio, considering it too steep, it would be worthwhile to review the proportions that should generate even greater concern. The National Association of School Psychologists recommends that a school district provide a psychologist for every five hundred students. In most states, however, there is one clinician for every two thousand students. There are some states in which the imbalance exceeds three thousand to one.

In 2014, the Cabarrus County School District in North Carolina had only one psychologist for every six thousand students. Imagine only three security guards at a Lakers game! Or worse, only three places to buy beer!

What kinds of outcomes can we reasonably expect when a single school psychologist is expected to get to know, diagnose, and treat 1,600 students (the national average)? And even these lopsided numbers are not painting an accurate picture. Often schools employ a psychologist for the purposes of being dedicated to a particular—typically small—group of special needs students.

Yet when numbers are reported, that clinician would be averaged into the entire student body. So it is fair to say that the ratio of psychologists to students is substantially less favorable than what is reported, which is nearly triple the rate recommended by the experts.

The picture does not get much rosier when we turn our attention to school counselors. The National Center for Education Statistics indicates that only five states meet the recommended student to counselor ratio of 250 to 1, which was established by the American School Counselor Association. According to a 2012 survey conducted by the College Board, the average high school counselor has 349 students in his or her caseload. Middle school counselors are tasked with juggling 415 raging conglomerates of hormones. When all age levels are considered, the national average of counselors to students is approximately 480 to 1.

Furthermore, school counselors have indicated that the majority of their day consists of handling the academic needs of students—schedules, credits, transcripts. Many are left without significant time to establish relationships with students or provide support for students' social and emotional needs. Nearly 900,000 students in this nation's schools do not even have access to a guidance counselor at all. Let's examine why this is such a big deal.

Over the past generation, cases of anxiety and depression have been on the rise. The National Institute of Mental Health reports that one in five children between the ages of thirteen and eighteen either have or will develop a mental health condition. Diagnoses can range from eating disorders and school phobia all the way to suicidal and homicidal ideation.

Some quick, back of the envelope calculations reveal that in an average school with one thousand students, two hundred have a mental health condition and—under optimal conditions—there are only six people (two psychologists and four counselors) trained to help them.

However, in forty-six states those numbers will be considerably more disproportionate. It is no small wonder that the National Alliance on Mental Illness has determined the average delay between the onset of a mental health disorder and prevention/care is ten years. Ten years! A typical school district only has a child for approximately thirteen years. Those are very thin margins within which to work.

With our current ratios, trees are falling in the woods but very few people are around to hear them. Therefore they must not be making many sounds—except for when the trigger hammers a metal pin into the backside of a bullet. Then it is loud and clear.

HOMICIDE AIN'T ALL

Tomorrow, if Congress revamped the Bill of Rights by repealing the Second Amendment and confiscating all of the nation's guns, increasing the number of counselors and clinicians would still be every bit as vital to the health and welfare of American children. The numbers indicate that the greatest danger facing kids is not the school shooter but rather the student him- or herself.

According to the Centers for Disease Control, suicide rates for males ages fifteen to nineteen has increased 31 percent over the past decade. Over that same time period it has doubled for females. Doubled. The five states with the highest rates of teen suicide are (in rank order) Alaska, Montana, New Mexico, Wyoming, and Nevada. They experience anywhere from 18.5 to 21.8 deaths per 100,000 people each year. When those figures are cross-referenced with the regional breakdown of counselors to students, we find that the West is the worst, with an average of 632 counselors for every pupil.

While there may not be causation, that should be enough smoke to make someone worry there might be a fire. At the very least, it should alert those statehouses to question why they employ less than half of the recommended number of school counselors and whether or not their children are paying the ultimate price for penny pinching. Overall, when we factor in death and the emotional trauma experienced by survivors, suicides lead to an annual loss of productivity of roughly $50 billion. So even for the heartless bean counters out there, it makes perfect financial sense to spend money on counselors and clinicians.

SUICIDE AIN'T ALL

If all of the guns were gone and no one ever committed suicide again, increasing the number of counselors and clinicians would still be an incredible use of our resources. According to a report published by Susan A. Carrell (a counselor) and Scott E. Carrell (a Dartmouth College professor), when counselors' caseloads drop from an average of 544 to 250—the number recommended by the American School Counselor Association—positive changes occur.

The number of incidents involving the recurrence of student discipline decreases by 25 percent. For minority and low-income students, the impact is even greater. The study shows that first-time disciplinary issues decrease as well. When students spend more time in the classroom and less in the in-school suspension room, it is a major victory for faculty morale, student self-esteem, and academic achievement.

FISHBOWL LIVING

If there were no guns, no shooters, no suicide, and no classroom behavior issues, increasing the number of counselors and clinicians would still be the greatest gift we could provide our students. This generation's young people are living in ways that parents just cannot understand. True, the Fresh Prince made a similar declaration nearly thirty years ago, but when we reassess through a modern lens, we see exactly how wrong he and Jazzy Jeff were.

Previous generations lacked the nuances of growing up in the next iteration of society. However, childhood near the end of the second decade of the twenty-first century is unlike anything ever. Sorry Mr. Fresh Prince.

When you mix uninformed/overwhelmed parents with techno-addictions with uninformed/in over their heads children with techno-addictions and unfettered access to too much too soon, you get a perfect storm of adolescent agony. As a result, we are producing a spate of lonely, helpless, angry, anxiety-ridden, fabulously well-informed, yet easily manipulated youth.

For every young person who utilizes technology to organize a fundraiser, befriend another halfway around the world, or shine a light on injustices foreign or domestic, there are several peers who are falling victim to the perils of technology and the new hyper-vindictive brand of pubescent socialization that has become commonplace in our communities.

"Some of these kids are mean." Have you heard that recently? Sometimes it is followed by the refrain, "Kids will be kids." While that certainly may be true, never before have they had the power to be the CEO of their own broadcast networks, programming hate speech in the form of tweets, snaps, memes, IMs, and videos, which run all day and all night. This content can range from mild banter to character assassination, from *Mickey Mouse Clubhouse* to *Game of Thrones.*

Middle school and high school social media may appear to be democratized and on a level playing field, but in fact they are not. These apps are weapons of propaganda in the hands of a manipulative oligarchy that somehow seizes authoritarian control over entire grades of children. Think North Korean TV, with the Dear Leader donning cool sneakers and a piercing.

Young men and women (mostly men) who are loners or "weird" are quickly labeled, with whispers of "next school shooter" swirling around their names. Social media allow those labels to proliferate, making these targets lonelier and subsequently angrier. Additionally, the internet allows these young, disenfranchised people to study the histories of past shooters in the privacy of their own phones, perhaps gleaning ideas or inspiration, as they may lack the tools to find their way out of these emotional rocky shoals.

So in that average school of one thousand students in which two hundred have/will develop a mental health disorder, how many of those issues will stem from the anxiety of living in a fishbowl? What about the other eight hundred, many of whom are struggling to balance a life of digital renown—constantly battling to make their lives appear more interesting to the judgmental masses who will unleash social network armageddon at the first whiff of weakness or ennui?

As the social network giant's endless barrage of emails suggest, "A lot has happened on Facebook since you last logged in." That just isn't true. Pretty much nothing has happened, but they are tapping into our society's newest anxiety: fear of missing out (FOMO). Twitter, Snapchat, and Instagram have their own ways of leveraging this same yearning.

Unfortunately it is working too well. So many have fallen victim to the trappings of living in the public eye, without any of the fortune, benefits, or choice tables at hot restaurants that used to come along with notoriety. To make matters worse, millions of children return home from school to a household of adults with their faces buried in devices of their own.

How many adults are modeling the destructive power of the web and social media with their profanity-laden tirades or derogatory remarks toward friends and strangers alike? Ironically, we have access to the most powerful communication tool in the history of forever and miscommunication is at an all-time high; civility is at an all-time low.

Counselors and clinicians trained in methods to deescalate and mediate conflicts, both practical and virtual, are worth their weight in gold. Even more valuable is their ability to impart coping skills to young people, who are woefully lacking in that department. This is undoubtedly a factor in the proliferating suicide rates.

Becoming well-adjusted does not occur in one or two seminal moments in the life of a child. Rather, it is the culmination of a million seemingly innocuous instances that test one's mettle: running out of your favorite cereal, a canceled play date, spilling the milk, having your TV/iPad/phone taken away, etc. That is why these specialists need ample time to have contact with students over a multitude of occasions, not just when the situation hits the fan.

It does not help that cyberbullies and trolls roam the web seeking to do harm. Twelve states have successfully passed a form of DASA legislation (Dignity for All Students Act), but identifying incidents of bullying after they occur is not enough. These harmful interactions need to be proactively disrupted. Once a nail is driven into a plank of wood, you can remove the spike, but the hole remains forever.

Schools need an army of counselors and clinicians, at more favorable ratios, to provide realistic opportunities for these critically important adults to get to know, work with, identify, and treat kids. When our nation looks to make gains in times of political discord, it trains and disseminates people who can build relationships, upon which it is our hope to move in a profitable direction.

Real gains do not only occur from drone strikes but from the diplomatic bonds formed in mud houses in Afghanistan and bunkers in Baghdad. This is where actual intelligence is gathered and potential dangers are identified.

In schools, this pivotal work starts in the PPS office. If districts are not spending money there, then they are simply lying to their communities by creating the illusion of increased safety while not changing a single substantive thing.

Chapter Ten

The Weaponization of Data

Like most other industries, education has recently fallen victim to the scourge that is Big Data. In the private sector, businesses have been stripped down to the studs and rebuilt utilizing Amazon-ified metrics to measure and micro target. This has catalyzed the reimagining of everything spanning from inventory to marketing. The upside is that the sweater you ordered with your cell phone while waiting to see the doctor you found on Zocdocs will arrive at your doorstep—according to real-time tracking—in just a short number of hours.

The downside is that every shred of privacy you once held dear has evaporated into the ether of the internet. In a forward fast world, tradeoffs are magnified. While Pandora's box (which predated the app, by the way) for the global marketplace may have opened permanently, schools can still rein in the demons before further damage ensues.

WELCOME TO THE THUNDERDOME

It is as though school leaders have suddenly found themselves in a furious, Mad Max–style death race to amass, analyze, and employ data to cure what ails our schools. Lest anyone need reminding, most of those cars burn up in fiery wrecks. So too will those who rely solely on quantitative data, such as graduation rates and test scores, to claim they can see into the soul of a school. Regrettably, this is exactly how mayors, governors, presidents, and state education departments purport to understand what they cannot comprehend. To steal a line from *MTV Diary*, "You think you know . . . but you have no idea."

In the early 1960s, when the New York Mets were woefully bad yet loveable nonetheless, a fan famously called a local paper to learn the results of a given day's game. When informed that the Mets scored nineteen runs against the Cubs, the fan replied, "Great! Did they win?" In March 2018, the United States Department of Education published a report claiming that high school graduation rates in the 2014–2015 school year reached a record 84 percent.

Great! But did they win?

Therein lies the problem with data—it is very easy to look at the wrong numbers and thereby draw the wrong conclusions. When lay people in charge of establishing policy, like politicians and Board of Education members, hear news such as the aforementioned graduation rates, they naively think that these diplomas were all earned the same way, with a consistent set of expectations applied evenly across the board.

Or worse, they know the hidden truth but would prefer to manipulate the meaning of these numbers to cast their education policies in a better light—a function of retaining their own power rather than empowering children. A look behind that 84 percent tells a different story.

In the same year that American high schools set records, 89 percent of districts offered at least one credit recovery course, which was up from 55 percent only five years earlier. Fifteen percent of all students in 2014–2015 actually participated in some form of credit recovery. Nearly one in six students!

For those who may be unaware, credit recovery is a strategy that allows students in danger of not graduating on time to earn credit in courses they have failed or possibly have never taken. Coursework is frequently condensed, with more and more programs having online or blended learning components. It is not uncommon for the preponderance of these courses to be taken in the months leading up to graduation.

Students who have recently emigrated with few, if any, transferable credits find great benefit in programs like this. For others, it is essentially an alternative pathway to graduation. Unlike the G.E.D., which is differentiated from a traditional diploma, those who make it through with the help of credit recovery are typically not distinguished from other students in, let's say, a report from the U.S. Department of Education declaring that educational outcomes are showing signs of improvement vis-à-vis graduation rates.

When the second largest school system in the nation, the Los Angeles Unified School District, elevated Michelle King to superintendent in January 2016, their most recent graduation rate was 72 percent. Three years and $45 million in credit recovery programs later, the number of high school students who crossed the finish line soared to 80 percent. Prior to stepping down for health reasons in 2018, Superintendent King regretted that she fell short of her goal of 100 percent. One hundred percent? That's quite a moonshot!

Even more interestingly, only 55 percent of those students who held diplomas bearing Ms. King's signature met the eligibility requirements to enroll in courses on the many U.C. campuses throughout the state of California. Essentially, nearly half of the students who met L.A.'s standards were ineligible to proceed to institutions of higher learning due to the skills they failed to procure while in the county's public schools.

These students represent the collateral damage that occurs when leaders chase data at all costs. It happens when those in control use a calendar to determine when a student is ready for commencement rather than accurately measuring that student's progress along a continuum of legitimate standards.

Is a high school diploma so valuable that we are willing to destroy its value in order to get more students across the finish line? One cannot help but wonder how many real educational benefits could have been enjoyed with that $45 million, which was misappropriated to allow certain individuals to boast about their visionary leadership.

Setting artificial graduation targets is akin to assigning police officers quotas for tickets or arrests. It places a premium on volume and repudiates quality. Conceptually, every teacher wants every child to succeed and meet/exceed standards, just like each member of law enforcement desires to bring all wrongdoers to justice.

Realistically, we understand that there are a multitude of factors that can impede on these lofty goals. Some are self-inflicted—such as retaining ineffective personnel—while some other facets are systemic or external, such as poverty, underfunded initiatives, and a loss of faith in our institutions to make good on their promises.

This is not unique to education or criminal justice. Just ask the good folks at Enron, Tyco, Facebook, Google, Hollywood accountants, every major bank, and many, many other companies. Each of these entities, to varying degrees, has unearthed ways to achieve artificial targets and milestones regardless of whether or not those pursuits involved jettisoning their moral compasses.

Similar to enhanced interrogation techniques, when you place enough pressure on your subordinates, you will eventually hear what you want to hear; it just may not reflect the truth. In a system as large and demanding as public education, many will choose self-preservation over all else, including what is best for kids.

WE SCARE BECAUSE WE CARE

Aside from graduation, the place where educators most commonly find themselves chasing data down the rabbit hole is with testing. Over the past two decades, teachers and students have endured a deluge of assessments from coast to coast. Thanks in large part to No Child Left Behind and Race to the Top, states have been incentivized to test and test and test in the hopes of amassing enough data to prove that either the system is working or it is broken. (It all depends on which side of the charter school/voucher debate one sits.)

To some degree, our educational complex has been set up like the scare factory in the Pixar film *Monsters, Inc.* Their city is powered by the literal screams of children. Our schools are powered by the figurative screams of young people being ushered through a Bataan Death March of endless assessments created by for-profit corporations and subsidized with the public's tax dollars. By the end of the film, the good monsters determine that joy and laughter are much more powerful than terror and sadness. Too many of our schools have yet to reach that same conclusion. Regardless, metastasizing testing leads to a host of problems.

First, when the school year is filled with assessments, it crowds out opportunities for authentic learning to occur. Teachers get caught in a vicious cycle of reviewing and testing, which consumes the calendar. This repetition also prompts students to ask the dreaded question, "Why do we need to know this?" Sadly, most topics covered in the classroom are ascribed value because they will appear on an examination or assessment of some sort and not because they serve a more meaningful purpose.

Not surprisingly, this strategy does not generate an intrinsic desire to learn on behalf of young people. It smacks of coercion, the most extrinsic and meaningless of motivators for the type of involvement and appreciation we seek to inculcate. Students quickly get numb from the bombardment, which leads to attendance and behavior issues. Teachers try to counter that loss of interest by hyping how important a test is, which eventually backfires. If all tests are important, then none of them are.

Despite the inauspicious nature of test escalation, various states and school systems have implemented a number of diverse strategies to raise assessment scores through increased teacher accountability. These methods can essentially be broken down into two categories: carrots and sticks. Both are flawed and awfully ineffective.

CARROTS

In the mid-2000s, the Atlanta Public Schools took a page from the corporate playbook and instituted merit pay for teachers and administrators whose students were able to meet certain targets on the Georgia Criterion-Referenced Competency Tests. And in full accordance with the laws of human nature—most notably greed—educators proceeded to uncover a multitude of ways for scores to rise illegitimately.

Their methods ran the gamut from seating weaker students near high achievers to facilitate cheating to "erasing parties," in which the adults manipulated answers on student test papers. This misconduct was allegedly prompted and encouraged by Dr. Beverly Hall, recognized as the National Superintendent of the Year in 2009.

Many were tried and convicted under racketeering laws typically reserved for members of organized crime. (Hall died before her trial concluded.) Their actions were immoral, unprofessional, and not completely unsurprising given the absurdity of what was expected.

There is a reason why a free market–style profit motive has been kept out of education—it leads to corruption. What happened in Atlanta was not unique; it was a high-profile mirror that allowed us to see the dangers of dangling carrots to raise test scores in our educational settings.

Practically every state has endured its own version of testing fraud. Many more instances have gone unreported, but make no mistake, wherever there is a bounty placed on higher test scores, cheating abounds. As we move forward fast into computerized testing, new opportunities to skew data and misrepresent student achievement will be contrived.

Can we once and for all cast aside the fallacy of merit pay? Educators are charged with, and tacitly accept, the challenge of maximizing the God-given potential of every single child, flaws and all. Therefore there is no need to further incentivize teachers and administrators with cash prizes. To do so invites in the devil to suppress our better angels—and teaching is an angel-driven business. Going above and beyond for students is the nature of the job. The greatest bonuses an educator can receive are fair wages, curriculum that makes sense, tests that are valid, and leaders who inspire.

STICKS

In 2013, the New York State Department of Education, under the direction of Commissioner John B. King Jr., responded to the federal Race to the Top program like a gunslinger setting out on horseback to collect reward money in the Wyoming Territory.

Wanted: Dead or Alive.

Rather than a double-barrel shotgun, King resorted to using an Annual Professional Performance Review (APPR) to bag his loot. In this take no prisoners, tyrannical beat down, educators were essentially told that either scores go up or they would end up on the endangered species list.

To make matters more complicated, this new system of measuring a teacher's worth was unveiled at the same time the state was rolling out massively flawed assessments to reflect the new Common Core Learning Standards. The confluence of these two events was damaging on a number of fronts.

APPR boosted morale in the teacher's lounge about as much as Alec Baldwin's visit to the sales office in *Glengarry Glen Ross*, the only exception being that Baldwin's character was at least offering a Cadillac to the winner. APPR, however, was a punishment-only program for both teachers and administrators.

Though New York State "won" $700 million for playing ball with Secretary Arne Duncan, very few schools saw any real financial benefits in the aftermath. A few short years later, Commissioner King had his ticket punched for Washington, DC, becoming Duncan's right hand. President Obama later anointed King Secretary of Education.

As the commissioner ascended, New York schools descended as a result of APPR, thanks in no small part to an unwelcomed onslaught of additional tests designed to measure student growth and, mysteriously, determine whether or not teachers "added value" to their students. Conveniently, Commissioner King provided a list of third-party vendors whose pre- and post-assessments were both legitimate for the APPR process and state-aidable. A wonderfully opportune coincidence.

Lawyers specializing in education did nicely during this time as a result of the many lawsuits filed against the state and the Department of Education to combat this unfair victimization of teachers. Grassroots parent groups responded by exercising a previously little-known clause permitting guardians to refuse testing.

In some parts of New York State, as many as 20 percent of students "opt out" of state assessments, practically delegitimizing the tests and sending the Department of Education's authority into a tailspin. To punch back, department brass began intimating that they would decrease public funding from those communities that withheld their children from exams.

Creating cultures of intimidation and fear has long been at the heart of a number of regimes from so-called reformers who manipulate data to spin tales of wonder and achievement . . . or miracles, like the one in Houston, Texas. Under Superintendent Rod Paige, the Houston Independent School District boasted truly incredible gains in testing and unbelievably low drop-out rates. These accomplishments were both incredibly impressive and absolutely fabricated.

For years, high school dropouts were intentionally coded incorrectly so they would appear as legitimate transfers, thus preserving stellar rates of graduation and "closing the achievement gap." For his efforts, Paige was named Secretary of Education by his former governor, President George W. Bush. In exchange, Bush claimed the mantle of "the education president."

One need not be a psychometrician to pick up on a pattern here: lead a large school system; make it appear effective on paper using lies, manipulation, depravity, racketeering, and coercion; get promoted. Nice work if you can get it.

While teacher and administrator accountability are absolutely essential, metadata will not lead us to that desired end. Numbers alone cannot tell the story of children or their schools any more than statistics can be the only metrics an experienced baseball manager uses to make decisions on the bench. Charts do not tell you whose swing looks good in the cage or who is a little off because his kid is sick or he is going through a divorce.

Great leaders need to be close enough to the people they shepherd to sense when the data are most applicable. People are incredibly complex and consistently defy attempts to be measured. Furthermore, if we continue to weaponize numbers, we are guaranteed to inflict damage upon many students and teachers who deserve much better. Perhaps the best use of metadata would be to find where the liars are and root them out of the system.

Those who remain should explore progressive ways to lead.

Chapter Eleven

Next-Gen School Leadership

Educators could learn a great deal from watching *Shark Tank*, the reality television show in which entrepreneurs pitch their products to a panel of wealthy investors in the hopes of procuring a well-heeled business partner in exchange for equity in their companies. The combined drama of rooting for the underdog and observing millionaires battling one another for a deal makes it easy to binge, for sure. But histrionics aside, devoted viewers will quickly deduce that most prospective agreements hinge on the answer to a single question: What is your competitive advantage?

In a world that has become so incredibly overcrowded with products offering similar, if not identical, benefits, it is more and more difficult to find anyone to invest in an idea that is simply good. We see this by the scores of previously optimistic business owners who walk, empty handed, down the long and lonely road out of the Shark Tank because there was nothing about their wares that stood out from others.

Education is suffering from a comparable dearth of differentiation and uniqueness, which can be attributed to traditional leadership principles rooted in a top-down organizational philosophy. In order for educators to unlock their competitive advantage, it will take leaders who employ wildly different strategies.

3 Rs FOR 4 Ps

For decades, the emphasis inside school houses has been on the "3 Rs": reading, writing, and arithmetic. (Why these are considered Rs when only one actually starts with that letter has always been a bit confounding.) This once laudable educational trifecta is in dire need of a modern makeover by

89

practitioners. Maximizing the potential of young people has everything to do with how we incorporate the 4 Ps to spark creativity and spur innovation into how students read, 'rite, and 'rithmetic.

According to educational researcher James Melvin Rhodes, nurturing the development of more creative individuals consists of identifying then cultivating four elements: Person, Process, Product, Press. Let's examine each in a school-related context.

1. Person

When educators and students walk into a school building each morning, they enter with varying states of mind. Some take a *veni, vidi, vici* approach, others are clock watching, and the rest fall somewhere in the middle. However, organizations that feature substantive levels of creativity and innovation are overwhelmingly composed of individuals willing to work harder and smarter and take risks. It is a convergence of Carol Dweck's growth mindset theory and Jay-Z's theorem of genius-level talent.

Creative people do not wait for divine intervention—or state mandates, superintendent directives, or principals' memos—to generate ideas. They recognize that wholehearted effort and focus on craft make all of the difference, and whatever setbacks or limitations they currently face can be overcome through perseverance, attention to detail, and the courage to march on.

In his masterwork *The World Is Flat*, Thomas L. Friedman perfectly captured this notion with the equation $CQ + PQ > IQ$. Friedman wisely asserted that, in the twenty-first century, the sum of one's curiosity and passion is greater than intelligence. In other words, it takes more than smarts these days.

In our forward fast world, the traditional landmarks of knowledge have either been moved or paved over, ushering us to a place where one's willingness to explore and persist can make all the difference. Book smarts are much less likely to beat out hustle when coupled with an unquenchable desire to see what is around the next corner. With a laptop you can change your world and possibly even the entire world. That kind of potential empowers people.

Therefore when young people proceed through their schooling years we must not only emphasize subjects and skills but also teach temerity, inquisitiveness, and resiliency. (You know, the "3 Ts.") These traits ought to be modeled, discussed, and supported across disciplines. Students need to feel the continuity room by room, period by period. Practice then praise. Practice then praise until it becomes the shared philosophy of the building.

2. Product

Creative people place great emphasis on what they are creating, whether it is shaping an idea, envisioning a new system, or developing a physical product. It is not a whimsical act. They proceed with careful consideration of how the product will be consumed and by whom. This does not mean that it is devoid of spontaneity, but the freedom to call audibles comes within the framework of what was intended. This helps inform the relationship between product and creator.

Think about a song. The product affords the creator an opportunity to articulate a particular thought or feeling through music and verse. It has a specific meaning that is dependent upon the maker's intentions. Once consumed, the song then takes on meaning to the listener, though sometimes in considerably unexpected ways. Bruce Springsteen's "Born in the U.S.A." is a perfect example.

We all develop varied relationships with the myriad products with which we interact, whether it be our computer, car, gaming system, stapler, or wristwatch. Some people go a bit overboard and develop rather unhealthy relationships with certain products (like cell phones or hair straighteners). Users rarely develop meaningful ties to products they feel any burden to consume. When was the last time you felt close to your engine air filter? It is only through coercion—buy it or your car will suffer—that any of us even make that purchase. This helps explain why corporations spend fortunes to market their merchandise.

An advertising campaign is nothing more than a fabricated narrative designed to offer a potential consumer an opportunity to envision him- or herself forming a positive relationship with a given good. Marketers, in actuality, are selling satisfaction; whenever possible they will amp up the ethos and logos, making the strongest appeals to our senses. Some products are more easily marketed to the heart and head, like candy, beer, cars, and food.

When strong, natural connections do not exist, like banking money can be a cold and distant object—ads will usually center on how a bank's services can help you pay for weddings, vacations, or retirements. While the cynic may argue that these methods are solely driven by capitalist lust, the end result is that successful producers are able to present products to consumers that project individualized end user creativity and innovation.

- With that MacBook, I will be able to write a book/learn to code/set high scores on games.
- With that Heineken, I will be able to bring friends together and make memories/forget about my ex-girlfriend/enjoy the game.
- With that Volvo, I will be able to keep my family safe/go on a road trip/ show everyone—especially my ex—that I can afford a nice foreign car.

Innately, we all wish to move our lives forward in some productive, satisfactory manner, which explains our susceptibility to effective marketing. Without products to aid us in the process of unlocking our fullest possibilities, one may perceive oneself as sentenced to a life of doldrums. It is at this exact place where our current educational model often breaks down.

Schools were originally built on the foundation of standardization. The intention was to maximize consistency and efficiency. We see it everywhere, from building design to classroom layouts, curricula/assessments, and the nearly identical calendar we all share. However, the Industrial Age that inspired all of this uniformity has ended. Eons of sameness have spawned an era of extreme differentiation.

Though we are using mostly the same digital tools, that hardware and software is allowing us to fashion environments centered on hyper-personalization. It isn't *a* phone or *the* phone, it is *my* phone. Incredibly, we can administer a state assessment in an arena format, instruct three hundred students to place their cell phones on tables near the entrance of the gymnasium, and at the conclusion of the exam, there isn't one student who confuses his or her phone with another.

We see this outside of technology as well. Have you tried counting how many craft beers and microbrews there are? Take a moment to notice the intricate ink of the tattooed masses. Long gone are the days of the carbon copy hearts, daggers, pythons, and tribal bands. Etsy, Pinterest, the slow food movement, phone accessories, photo filters, eyelashes on headlamps, etc. are all attempts by individuals to create their own microcosms of distinctiveness in a world dominated by a handful of oligopolies. But homework has remained unchanged. That's a problem.

When school leaders require teachers to teach the same old curriculum, in the same old ways, in preparation for the same old tests, it takes a sledgehammer to innovation. That is one of the downsides of coercion-based standardization. Likewise, when teachers structure lessons and assignments with similar expectations of conformity, they should expect their students to exhibit a comparably diminished desire to engage in homogenized work.

Furthermore, if we provide students with digital tools capable of producing unique and deeply personalized work, then direct them to complete cookie-cutter assignments designed with uniformity in mind, we are going to confuse the heck out of them. Effective leaders recognize that clarity is one of the key elements to shaping a vision and increasing buy-in. Ambiguity is anathema to success.

Placing an emphasis on Product will not require educators to abandon their successful methods of the past but rather incorporate a newfound flexibility through which they can widen the net and inspire more students to uncover personalized connections to the disciplines they are learning and the work they are producing.

No longer will students and teachers feel compelled to simply check boxes and go through the motions on their way to report cards and W-2s. Rather, this approach can help unlock the creative potential of both instructor and pupil, promoting heightened intentionality and purpose while establishing a vibrant learning community inside of the classroom.

3. Process

"Early on, all of our movies suck."

Given the largely unparalleled success of their films, both critically and financially, it may seem a bit surprising that this profoundly honest confession is attributed to one of Pixar's founding fathers Ed Catmull. This remark rather bluntly captures the early stages of creativity. At their inception, ideas are almost always crude and considerably messy—like babies. It is not until the nurse cleans up the newborn and swaddles him or her in a blanket that a parent can say, "Phew. I was worried there for a second."

Catmull goes on to offer an incredibly succinct explanation of the trials and tribulations of Process: "Our job is to make movies go from suck, to not suck." He makes no mention of lightning bolts or signs from heaven. His team recognizes the practicality of Edison's mantra—perspiration far outweighs inspiration—and employs it with aplomb.

Quite often, innovation comes down to just you and a blank piece of paper or empty computer screen. Whether you are a filmmaker or an educator, that can be daunting. Without faith in one's process, that silent cursor can drive a person into submission, like the harrowing beat in "The Tell-Tale Heart." This notion resonates with those who spend countless hours creating their own lessons and professional learning opportunities.

Wanting to do a great job to both satisfy one's professional obligations and make a difference in the lives of kids is only the first step of the journey. Finding a method of moving oneself through the process of creation and innovation is an even weightier task. Ideally, every instructional idea is subjected to that process, so it can become a part of you and so parts of you are present in all of the work that you do. This requires tremendous effort and focus. Nothing worth anything is easy.

This understanding of Process helps clue us in as to why canned curriculum customarily fails to bring about the leaps in student achievement that were promised at the time a given program was purchased. It does not necessarily reflect poorly on the materials themselves (though that can certainly play a role), but educators delivering instruction using prefab lessons have very little skin in the game. Photocopying, scanning, and uploading are not substantial elements of Process. Those actions greatly diminish a teacher's creative capacity and foster dispassionate learning habitats.

Lo and behold, the aforementioned program is abandoned because it produced underwhelming results after a short period of implementation. (Why such a brief time? Because someone on the leadership front—Board, superintendent, principal—must show that decisive steps are being taken to address the given deficiencies, even if they do not necessarily understand what the actual problems or solutions truly are.) The program is quickly replaced with another, usually costly, program that comes with even loftier assurances of success. ("This time we got it right!")

Despite good intentions, there is a significant likelihood that this district's new initiative will fail to yield the desired results as well. In this scenario, the problem plaguing the district is not personnel, programs, or the willingness to pull the trigger, it is Process.

Educators need time to figure out how to go "from suck, to not suck." Jumping from one math program to another without allowing smart people to internalize shortcomings, innovate, and turn weaknesses into strengths makes as much sense as Pixar abandoning an entire film because they are unhappy with a particular plot point.

The same flaws in Process that obstruct a single school building or an entire school system from tapping into its greatest innovative and creative potential frequently show up in classrooms as well. Sometimes the very teachers who wish to be untethered from mandates so they can spread their wings are the same individuals who insist upon uniformity and adherence to a strict set of teacher-constructed guidelines from their students. This juxtaposition is not dissimilar to how certain educators demand respect and attention from their classes but are disrespectful and inattentive at meetings and workshops. What's that saying about the goose and the gander?

Many of our students are Porsches and Lambos, but curiously we insist upon only taking them for a ride in the school parking lot. By dedicating the necessary time to Process and preaching the importance of method, intention, and purpose, we can transport young people to the Autobahn, where they can open up the throttle of their cognitive and imaginative minds.

4. Press (Place)

A lot of attention has been paid in recent years, to how Silicon Valley companies are designing their employees' workspaces. Layouts run the gamut from open floor plans to situating bathrooms in one specific location, funneling traffic and promoting impromptu meetings or "happy accidents" (pardon the bathroom humor) among personnel. Many of these campus-like offices also offer free food, dry cleaning, toys, scooters, Ping-Pong tables, and a bevy of other perks to keep everyone content, motivated, and, most importantly, remaining at work for extensive amounts of time.

While that is certainly an element of Press, Rhodes's fourth and final "P" goes beyond the physical plant. It speaks to the environment established by the leaders of an organization—how they endorse a particular philosophy that is supportive of creativity and innovation on behalf of individuals and collaborative teams. School administrators working with shrinking budgets can rest assured that this does not require cool furniture and popcorn makers, though they would be fun and probably appreciated. Press is about establishing an attitude of empowerment and evoking institutional climate change for the betterment of all.

So how do we accomplish that?

In his work on regulatory focus theory, Columbia University psychology professor E. Tory Higgins argues that there are two ways in which a person can be persuaded to attain a desired goal. Through a *promotion focus*, an individual strives to achieve, considering the work necessary to fulfill an aspirational objective or ambition. When a person adopts a *prevention focus*, he or she is attempting to accomplish a task out of a sense of obligation or fear of punishment. Each focus correlates to vastly different emotional responses or states of mind.

Coaches of competitive or professional teams have to choose between these two foci all the time. In their attempt to get the best from their athletes, they may say something like, "If you can't do the job, someone else will take your place." In this case, the player will seek to play well for the purpose of self-preservation (prevention focus). Or perhaps that coach tells the same individual, "This is your chance to make an important contribution to our team." Now the athlete has a sense of duty to team and to self (promotion focus). Additionally, in the latter scenario, the player feels the support of his or her coach, which can strengthen their bond through both success and failure.

So as you may have already inferred, regulatory focus theory is constructed atop the premise that people tend to move toward pleasure and away from pain. This instinctual approach tends to increase levels of contentedness and motivation. Quite simply, we want to experience more of what makes us feel good and less of what hurts. However, we often lack the autonomy to choose which focus we prefer. In an organization like the public school system, promotion and prevention foci not only come in the form of directives but are also determined by the environment established by its leaders.

In a system this large it is very easy for the average educator to point fingers and disavow any responsibility for a school climate mired in a prevention focus. Because everyone has a boss, you may hear the familiar refrain, "Oh, if it weren't for the _____ (fill in the blank with curriculum director, assistant principal, principal, superintendent, Board of Education, department of education, president of the United States), I would be able to do more/do better/do anything." Of course there is some validity here, but only to a certain degree.

In actuality, anyone at any one of these management levels could take decisive action by breaking the cycle of self-preservation and self-aggrandizement through coercion. However, they unfortunately prefer to allow bad habits that are in motion to remain in motion.

The propensity to imitate the counterproductive tone established "from above" typically arises from one or more of the following: frustration, disillusionment, deception, laziness, or lack of confidence in one's ability to make a difference. That demonstrates the power of negativity and anxiety.

This behavior also harkens back to a familiar time when good leadership was determined by top-down organizational flow charts depicting who must kowtow to whom. But we have moved forward fast and have the technological tools and collaborative mindsets to break away from precedent.

Following the mantra "success leaves clues," let us explore a place in which people are moving forward even faster and, arguably, across greater institutional, societal, and cultural distances than educators: Iran.

Imagine how difficult it must be to motivate and change the mindsets of individuals whose very identities are deeply entrenched in past practices dating back to the seventh century. Yet they have embarked on a journey to develop their businesses and markets to compete in a frenzied, fast-paced, interdependent, modern world.

In 2016, postdoctoral fellow at the University of Tehran Ashkan Khalili investigated transformational leadership practices across a number of Iranian industries and identified the following six key behaviors that promoted the greatest levels of creativity and innovation among more than one thousand employees:

1. Articulation: providing employees with a vision of the future that is compelling.
2. Intellectual stimulation: challenging employees to rethink how they do their work.
3. Modeling: leaders act as role models, demonstrating the principles and values that are important to the organization.
4. High expectations: employees are counted upon to perform at a distinguished level.
5. Accepting group goals: foster cooperation and support outcomes.
6. Individualized support: take employees' feelings into consideration.

This transformation paradigm is much more robust and prosperous than "Hassan, you work for me and what I say goes." These behaviors help foster and sustain workers who engage in creative and innovative solutions to the problems they encounter in their day-to-day responsibilities rather than waiting for directives. It leads to enhanced positive associations with critical, time-sensitive tasks, helping individuals overcome fears, increase productivity, and lead more invigorating, satisfying professional lives.

This is a far cry from those whose work environments project a prevention focus. Those folks are likely to tap out as soon as the task is completed. They do not want to experience those unpleasant feelings a second time, if humanly possible. These involuntary responses to stimuli are part of our genetic makeup—move toward pleasure and away from pain. Why do you think Nabisco sells all of those Oreos?

It would be wonderful to have armies of superintendents and principals not only espousing the value of promotion focus but also practicing these six transformational leadership behaviors with their faculties. Teachers would be inspired to become the most creative, innovative versions of themselves. The atmospheric metamorphosis in buildings would be palpable. However, while we all sit and wait for Godot, there is something even more powerful that educators could start doing right away: turn every classroom into its own micro-organization.

If Khalili's six behaviors of transformational leadership can turn out positive change in the boardrooms of Tehran, isn't it worth trying in the classrooms of Topeka? Or Tallahassee? Or Tacoma?

Imagine schools in which teachers, counselors, and clinicians move beyond considering themselves educators and embrace the notion that they are educational *leaders* who wield immense power—classroom CEOs, if you will. Through the adoption of a promotion focus, they could help minimize or even eliminate the very characteristics of prevention focus (fear, anxiety, negativity, top-down management) that lead to either grade-induced coercion or low levels of academic engagement/achievement on behalf of students. After all, like their adult counterparts, children move toward pleasure and away from pain.

Young people not only need to be taught, they also need to be inspired. Yet too often that aspect is overlooked due to the machinations of the mighty and the misinformed. Directives to place limits on children abound. On the first days of school, they are reminded—ad nauseum—of all the behaviors they cannot demonstrate. While one can argue that going over rules is a "necessary evil," a person entering into an organization would much prefer someone—a leader or teacher—to articulate a compelling vision of the future.

Individuals desire to explore ways to rethink how they go about completing their work. They want leaders to act as role models. They long to exist in an environment in which all participants are embodying the values of the organization. They yearn to be supported. Last and most importantly, they pray for a boss who will take their feelings into consideration. As Teddy Roosevelt once remarked, "Nobody cares how much you know, until they know how much you care."

So once classroom CEOs adopt a promotion focus, what is the next step?

CLIMATE CHANGE

With the winds of change blowing across so many school campuses, the battle for supremacy between new ideas and past practices is in full tilt. The manner in which school leaders handle this pivotal time will reverberate well into the future of education. To help refine the complexity of making decisions in this frenzied yet formidable era of unparalleled technological advancement, consider framing everything around two simple questions:

Why?

Why not?

Both questions can provoke fear or evoke excitement. Both questions can help schools navigate through uncharted territory. Both questions appear childishly simple yet can unearth an intricate web of complexities. The most vexing part will be to figure out when to ask which question.

WHY?

Since the birth of cinema, movie images were captured on some type of film, which was later developed, edited, color corrected, and printed. The physical presence of film was so essential that the entire industry was bestowed with that name. From box office juggernauts to small, arthouse indies, only one standard existed. This held true even when 16mm film stock was so cost prohibitive that a guerrilla filmmaker like Robert Rodriguez would have to literally sell his body to science to cover the $7,000 budget of his first film, *El Mariachi.*

Then technology walked through the door.

Suddenly, movie makers had the ability to shoot almost endless amounts of footage, with fewer lights, slashed production costs, nominal editing expenses—thanks to nonlinear methods that didn't involve cutting the negative—and not one inch of film needed to be developed in a lab. It was a dream come true. But here's the ironic part: the industry shunned them.

That's right. People who love making films thumbed their collective noses at those who found new tools with which to explore their storytelling talents. When "purists" respond in this fashion, it is usually rooted in one thing: fear of change.

Speaking on this topic before a crowd of experienced and aspiring artists, Rodriguez—one of the earliest mainstream adopters of digital filmmaking—told the following story in his defense of abandoning the beloved celluloid. One day, Rodriguez watched as his wife prepared a ham dish that he loved. He noticed that she cut the ends off prior to placing the ham in the pan. When questioned as to why she would discard those pieces, Rodriguez's wife shrugged, explaining that this was her mother's recipe.

So Rodriguez approached his mother-in-law to inquire about that particular aspect of the preparation. After pondering for a moment, mom confessed that she had no idea why the ends of the ham were disposed of prior to baking. She informed Rodriguez that this was *her* mother's recipe. So Rodriguez paid a visit to grandma. Upon posing this question to *abuela*, the family matriarch sheepishly replied that years ago the only pan she owned was very small, so in order to fit the ham inside she had no choice but to cut the ends off.

This allegory explains the importance of not shying away when it comes to asking Why. Often even the finest practitioners lose sight of the reasons behind certain traditional methodologies. It is akin to how we no longer feel a pencil when it is in our hands. Patterns and habits become so ingrained in our daily rituals that any departure from certain norms not only feels awkward but also unnatural. However, the reality is that we now possess larger pans.

Thanks to digital tools, our ability to collaborate and share ideas with professionals near and far has magnified our potential to do so much more. The power of Why allows us to explore the limitations of the pan we *have*, not the pan we *had*.

Of course, asking Why does not guarantee that something must change. Sometimes there are perfectly valid reasons for certain practices to be as they are. The very best way to substantiate the rationale for maintaining the status quo is by challenging it. If a given practice can withstand the scrutiny, it is legitimized.

For the betterment of an organization, this type of regular reflection and assessment helps bring everyone together on the same page. It also engenders trust that change won't be made flippantly or merely for the sake of change, as it so often comes to pass.

Perhaps the most important reason to ask Why is to promote an institutional philosophy that change is not feared. It also acknowledges that nothing is set in stone—learning environments ought to be fluid, in the sense that they respond to the changes that accompany society and, most importantly, the life experiences of our students.

- Why do we still structure the school day this way?
- Why do we teach certain curricula and not others?
- Why do we assess students in particular formats/modalities?

- Why do we ring bells?
- Why do we give homework?
- Why do we fill our classrooms with the same furniture?
- Why do we still teach _____?
- Why? Why? Why?

It is crucially important to remember, for the sanity of the students and faculty of a school, that simply asking Why should not always precipitate change. Sometimes continuity and precedent reflect the high standards and best practices we all seek. Environments that feature everyone jumping on the "Why Bandwagon" at every whim will produce untenable levels of disruption. Exploring the merit of an organization's intentions, systems, and consequences is healthy, but a scorched earth policy of the past is not.

Once we have finished exploring Why, the next challenge is arguably even more important in a forward fast world.

WHY NOT?

The easiest and safest decision for an educational leader to make is to say no. Entire careers have been built off of this single word. If you survived last year relatively unscathed, the most logical and job-secure action you can take is to do your darndest to do nothing different. The longer you hold to this principle, the more you establish precedent, which spawns stagnation for the sake of longevity. Just about the dumbest, most personally irresponsible question you can ask is Why Not?

So how can we inspire people to ask it?

While Why affords us a chance to reimagine the past, Why Not challenges us to dream up the future. After we contemplate Why, we can always safely retreat to past practice and gently remove our necks from the guillotine before the level is pulled. Why Not potentially strands us on an island inhabited by the producers of *John Carter* and the proponents of New Coke. Why Not exposes us to the slings and arrows of I told you sos and what were you thinkings.

At the same time, Why Not is the very first question that preceded anything worth anything in this world. And we need brave souls in education, now more than ever, willing to go there and take the necessary risks on behalf of children.

- Why not teach _____?
- Why not configure the day differently?
- Why not bring technology into instruction?
- Why not infuse New Literacy Studies?

- Why not assess students in brand new ways?
- Why not give children more autonomy?
- Why not give teachers more autonomy?
- Why not close down _____ and open up _____?

Why Not takes the mantra "failure is not an option" and sets it on its ear. As we move forward fast, failure most certainly is an option. It is practically an inevitability. Educators, parents, and school Boards must recognize that there are valid reasons to fail and that, if we are failing correctly, each failure brings us one step closer to the right answer. Those right answers bring our institutes of learning to a far, far better place academically, socially, and emotionally.

Technology companies have a very practical understanding of this concept. When innovators launch software, apps, websites, and games, they do so in a beta format. There is recognition that the known unknown will eventually surface and need to be remedied. In the old days, when the disk you purchased arrived in a box (that was always comically larger than it needed to be, by the way), that was it—for better or for worse. The only solutions we had were blowing into the Atari cartridge or wiping the installation disk on our shirt. If that didn't solve the problem we were out of luck.

Today it is a different story. Bugs and errors are constantly being identified, worked around, and injected wirelessly into the mainline. New versions continually add functionality and features to the programs we already utilize—sometimes to our satisfaction and other times to give us additional gray hairs. These advances can only occur if the creators listen to feedback, reflect on what they have created, and continue to ask Why Not when it comes to improving their creation. This leads to further exploration and products that are more robust for users.

For years, the educational equivalent of this was "data-driven instruction." Essentially, teachers and building leaders were asked to look at grades and test scores, then figure out how to make them go up. The toolbox available to raise achievement was extremely limited and quickly became rote, like using shampoo: lower class size, increase extra help/labs, add professional development, repeat. Though these limitations were sometimes induced by a lack of resources, the real culprit was a dearth of risk taking and creativity.

Over time, class sizes creep back up, labs disappear or are used for "double notes," and professional development feels like yet another iteration of *NCIS*. (This time it takes place in Boston, ooh . . .) Before long, someone sees a statistic that is troubling, then calls for the old toolbox to be brought out and the cycle begins anew. As soon as the needle moves a little in the intended direction, the leaders breathe a sigh of relief because, once more, they narrowly escaped failure. This is somehow mistaken for success.

Perhaps University of Florida football coach (Go Gators!) Dan Mullen summed up this flawed mindset best:

> I think sometimes we're looking at the guys' eyes and they're coming in this program and they fear losing and they're relieved by winning. And you can't be successful that way. You can't play that way, you can't act that way, you can't even think that way. You've got to go out there and go so hard because you love to win.

Mullen encourages his players to hate losing but not fear it. This fosters a greater confidence and resiliency in themselves and their teammates. Emphasizing risk taking and positive growth without admonishing well-intentioned mistakes could make for a very powerful school climate. And it can all begin by asking Why Not?

AD IN

In a system originally designed for conformity, deviation was not regularly encouraged. Look no further than how we attire our graduating classes; individualism is marginalized, suggesting that graduates are no more than the output of a large machine, with teachers and administrators serving as its interchangeable cogs, churning out degree holders. It is no small wonder students have such a burning desire to decorate their caps—it is their only opportunity to differentiate themselves. Vibrant organizations challenge members to apply their individual talents and perspectives, to reinvent their roles and contribute in a collaborative manner to the greater good.

The future of education isn't in any textbook or Google or Apple in-service training course. It resides in the creative and innovative minds of education's most important practitioners: teachers and administrators.

This brings us back to *Shark Tank*. Considering how critical it is to establish one's competitive advantage, school leaders should dig deep and figure out what sets their school apart from the rest other than colors and a mascot. Those are merely identifiers—fodder for bumper stickers and sweatshirts. The purpose of a promoting your competitive advantage is to get others—teachers, community members, etc.—to *invest* in your product.

However, the elevator pitch does not end in the principal's office. To achieve success in the classroom, teachers rely upon students to make an investment in them as well. But if all you have to offer is the required textbook, the district curriculum, and the state assessment, you may as well be peddling "cola." Do not be surprised to find very few, if any, offers from the thirty-plus Sharks contemplating your proposal.

Like most good investors, young people heavily guard their precious resources until they see a road to profitability. So if you put forward something compelling and uniquely yours, more people will be willing to ante up and go along for the ride.

Chapter Twelve

Backward Fast

The preceding chapters discussed ways for educators to reimagine the present and make meaningful strides in our forward fast schools. However, there are some practices and methods in which schools continue to engage that not only impede upon our forward progress but are perhaps moving us in the wrong direction altogether. We can ill afford negative growth at such a critical juncture. Let's take a moment to shine a light on some educational constructs that should work, maybe have worked, but no longer work as intended.

COMPUTER-BASED TESTING

Perhaps this sounds incredibly hypocritical given how the crux of this book promotes technology in education, but there is an explanation. For more than a decade, for profit test makers have been fruitlessly trying to crack the code of computer-based testing (CBT) and bring all of our schools on board. In that same decade, the United States recovered from the Great Recession, Sidekicks and flip phones were supplanted by web-enabled, portable computers capable of facial recognition and augmented reality, same-sex marriage became legal, and the Chicago Cubs won the World Series. How is it that in a decade in which the unimaginable became reality, CBTs are still being "phased in?"

For starters, CBTs are problematic in a number of logistical ways. How many mornings do you walk into your school building and hear, "Network's down," "Email's down," or "Phone's down." Though we rely on infrastructure, we must concede that it is not always reliable. As we know from the Ten Truths about Tech, technology will let you down when you need it most.

In the case of CBT, it will be the day three hundred students show up to take the biggest exam of their lives. That gives administrators pause—and rightly so.

Second, different school districts have approached technological implementation using vastly disparate philosophies. A handful were early adopters, handing out tablets with dedicated classroom carts or on a 1:1 basis, while others allowed students to BYOD. Some districts came along somewhat later, while the *Leave It to Beaver* contingent viewed technology as the spawn of Satan and prohibited these gadgets altogether.

Among the schools that chose technology, some went with touchscreens, while others opted for keyboards. For some, digitization has become the standard for classroom learning, while in other classrooms devices serve as glorified notebooks or expensive paperweights. This varies by district, school, and classroom.

When you factor in all of these juxtaposed elements, it becomes easier to understand the operational difficulties of implementing CBTs. Not to mention, new rules have to be written to govern issues like when batteries die in the middle of a test, restarting individualized timers after bathroom breaks, screens that inexplicably freeze, techno-phobic exam proctors, and "HAL 9000 Moments" when the computer develops a mind of its own and inadvertently sabotages a student's work.

Even more challenging is the human element. Makers of these exams tout how their products accommodate special needs students, and they do to an extent. However, with CBTs, we bear witness to yet another instance of technologists who erroneously believe that they have successfully circumvented the need for personal interaction. There are those young people with coordination or motor skills deficiencies who may find great difficulty with CBTs and require the guiding hand of an exam administrator.

Although a CBT can read questions and answer choices aloud, the monotony of hearing a synthesized voice over the course of an entire exam can become quite taxing on any student, especially students with sensory issues. Furthermore, the testing software will never be able to gauge the temperament of a child or pick up on the visual cues suggesting that a special needs student is frustrated or at the breaking point.

There are many times when proctors sense that a water break, an encouraging pat on the shoulder, or a quick supervised stroll around the hallway can help a child emotionally reset, regaining the composure and focus needed to continue. Which tab are you supposed to click for that?

For a moment, let us give these companies the benefit of the doubt and imagine that we invest the time, energy, and monetary resources needed to work out all of the aforementioned technological, logistical, and emotional components. When you look at prominent CBTs, like the PARCC exam, you find that they are virtually no different than the paper version of assessments students have been taking forever. Read the passage, then click on the choice that best answers the question. Analyze the equation, then solve for *x*. Except now when you find *x*, type the value in the text box.

Is this the breakthrough in testing we have been waiting for?

There is very little point in using twenty-first-century technology to test twentieth-century skills. Having access to some more assessment data is hardly worth the investment required to make CBTs a reality in every school. With modern scanning and analytics tools, we have more than enough data to know what is going on with our students.

However, if we could adopt those same devices to assess knowledge and skills that can only be demonstrated through the use of technology, *that* would be a game changer. In other words, CBTs need to be reimagined to reflect where we are going rather than where we have been. We do not need to go from "been there, done that" to "been there, done that on a tablet." There is so much more.

How well can students find useful resources on the web?

How thoroughly do they analyze the validity of those sources?

To what extent can they code? Design web pages? Design apps?

To what extent can they identify and articulate violations of internet ethics?

How efficiently and effectively can they create a web tutorial and post it?

How adequately can they utilize technology to build, create, innovate, and collaborate?

You know, actual twenty-first-century skills.

Note to test makers: Give educators the CBTs they desire or prepare to waste another decade piloting your products.

ISLANDS IN THE STREAM

Some years back, several well-intentioned educators set schools on a wild goose chase that continues to this day. Cashing in on how much everyone loves acronyms, districts launched the first S.E.M. initiatives. Of course, science and math had been cornerstones of students' academic programs for generations, but this new educational philosophy would introduce courses in engineering as well.

The notion was built upon the precept that young people would be better prepared for college and careers if they possessed a background in these three essential, related disciplines. That is sound reasoning and a very viable concept, which means someone eventually has to come along and ruin it.

"What do you mean you are only doing S.E.M.?" says Sally Superintendent, a classic one-upper, who loves getting her picture in the local paper. "Our district has recently launched a brand new initiative called S.*T*.E.M. because we believe that technology is at the heart of everything our youngsters will experience in higher education and, ultimately, the workforce." Just like that, the gauntlet is thrown at the feet of other superintendents, educational policy makers, and learning science researchers. They immediately crank up the professional development machine because everyone is going to need training in S.T.E.M. A.S.A.P.

Flash forward eighteen months later . . .

Your superintendent is at a conference somewhere in a galaxy far, far away. He or she feels good knowing that his or her S.T.E.M. initiative, though initially challenging to fund and get faculty buy-in, has finally turned a corner and is starting to become part of the district's culture.

And then it happens . . .

He sits down in a cavernous hotel meeting room filled with other educational leaders and is immediately enraptured by a prominent professor orating from the lectern about the world-changing power of S.T.E.*A*.M. It turns out the latest, latest research indicates that the lynch pin in preparing students for the twenty-first century is the arts. "The arts! How could we have missed that?" your superintendent confesses to no one as he facepalms over his omelet. S.T.E.M. is just not enough. Within minutes, he opens his laptop and fires off a salvo to his second in command, who was given the pleasure of staying back to mind the store:

> Crank up the professional development machine. We're transitioning to S.T.E.A.M. Oh, and find out how much it costs to fly in this professor. He's terrific!

Two years later. . . .

Your superintendent regrettably ascends to that big central office in the sky. However, he leaves behind his legacy: S.T.E.A.M. As it turns out, the arts really do make all the difference. Kids are succeeding and morale is high. All is well, until you attend the Opening Day Conference and meet your new leader, who boasts of many successes in her prior post: Sally Superintendent. She has big news. Starting today, the district will be launching an exciting new initiative called—you guessed it—S.T.*R*.E.A.M.

See the latest, latest, latest research assures us that what is really missing in a quality twenty-first-century education is reading. Oh . . . and writing. So the acronym should actually be: S.T.R.W.E.A.M. Wisely, Sally Superintendent elects not to use this spelling as it would likely cause a spike in speech therapy.

For years, *writing* has been considered an *R* word, so maybe this initiative should be referred to as S.T.R.R.E.A.M.? Then again, *arithmetic* is also an *R* word, and that is technically the same thing as *math*. So the acronym really should read S.T.R.R.E.A.R. Maybe we ought to simply tell students we are putting them under A.R.R.E.S.T? Wait, I'm missing an *R*. . . .

Can we all please agree to step off of this hamster wheel?

What all of these initiatives are intending to achieve is the establishment of robust, modern learning environments capable of preparing our students to meet with success in the future. So let us stop wasting time with perpetually expanding buzzwords and catchphrases and channel that energy (and money and time and human capital and goodwill) into making forward fast schools a reality in every neighborhood—creating an acronym-free world of new possibilities and opportunities for every child.

THE TROUBLE WITH TENURE

Much like the dreaded kitchen table sit down with mom, when you find out where babies really come from, it is time to have a grown-up conversation—this time about tenure. Quite frankly, on a systemic level, there is no hardware, software, smart device, reading program, testing initiative, curriculum redesign, professional development workshop, or organizational epiphany that will ever overcome the detriment of tenure on our schools. (Okay, so the Band-Aid has been ripped off. Now for the rationale.)

First, it is essential to clarify that these feelings toward tenure should not be misinterpreted as a disdain of labor unions. On the contrary, educators need to fight harder than ever to ensure our right to collectively bargain and stand shoulder to shoulder in professional unity. This must never be infringed upon or diminished, not one iota. The clarion call for unions to be disbanded has intensified as some statehouses have slowly but surely chipped away at what was sacrosanct for more than a century.

But let us not conflate tenure with union, as nearly every other organized labor group exists without tenure. Those associations exhibit every bit of strength while incorporating reasonable rules and regulations that govern the termination of individuals who do not meet professional standards and expectations. It is not, however, ironclad. For all intents and purposes, tenure is and that is highly problematic.

According to a study conducted by the National Center for Education Statistics, approximately one in every five hundred tenured teachers is dismissed. Essentially, 99.8 percent of tenured teachers have, to put it in U.S. Supreme Court parlance, a lifetime appointment. That is even purer than Ivory soap.

The average school district in the United States has 187 educators. If only the single least effective, lowest-performing individual were removed, that would translate to a dismissal rate of roughly 0.5 percent, more than double the actual number. Would it be considered a harbinger of doom if a paltry 99.5 percent of tenured teachers were retained?

The fact remains that both of these statistics are embarrassingly unrealistic relative to every other profession. Those who side with the plaintiff in the case of *Vergara v. California* have argued—unsuccessfully—that tenure is harmful to students, especially those in high-poverty regions. School Board members bemoan the exorbitant expense and number of years required to pursue—not even ensure—a due process dismissal under the current regulations. Neither of these arguments is the most compelling reason to eliminate tenure.

The real disservice of tenure is that it can promote irrational behavior on behalf of those who have it and those who seek it. For the seekers:

- There are some people who select this profession because of the allure of tenure. For them, it is even more compelling than being off for the summer. Neither is a valid reason to embark on one of the most important career paths in our society.
- It is not uncommon for teachers to demonstrate certain highly professional and responsible behaviors during their probationary years, only to abandon them upon procuring tenure. Sadly, a handful even has the gall to boast about all of the uncharacteristic behaviors they plan to demonstrate once their interim period is completed. These can range anywhere from punctuality and attendance to lack of adequate preparation or even maintaining personal hygiene.
- Too often, tenure is dictated by the calendar. The state in which a neophyte is employed will determine if he or she is deemed "good enough to keep forever" in two, three, or four years. How many quality instructors, with worlds of potential, have been released because the hour glass ran out of sand?

And if a principal wishes to extend the probationary status of someone with potential, he or she is typically grilled for failing to conform to a predetermined time frame. As a result, districts adopt philosophies like, "When in doubt, get them out." That is not in the best interest of a new teacher who may require additional opportunities to learn and develop. This is especially true in forward fast learning environments. With so many stops and starts of various technological initiatives, it potentially undermines the growth of a new teacher who has an incredibly narrow window to "get it right."

Conversely, how many times does it break the other way, where individuals are pushed through and granted tenure because the clock ran out on ineffective administrators who failed to adequately train or properly document the shortcomings of a relatively unskilled or unqualified educator?

Sometimes regime change can knock struggling probationers off the radar screen, allowing them an opportunity to back in to tenure without truly satisfying any particular set of requirements or demonstrating desired growth. Once again, this places an unfair burden on the highly skilled teachers who must now try to compensate for a colleague who is ill prepared to competently satisfy his or her professional responsibilities for the next thirty years or more.

For those who have tenure:

- Even the finest educators can be lulled into a sense of complacency; former go-getters may grow content with mediocrity. It isn't difficult to see why. In any facet of life, youthful exuberance can give way to ennui over time. Education is no exception. When you factor in a very rigid pay scale, with predictable (and often minimal) increases, along with the ceaseless repetition of one school year rolling into the next, people can find themselves wanting for inspiration. Tenure has the ability to exacerbate this dilemma for a number of reasons.

1. The Mastery Trap

Once an educator has reached the tenure mountaintop, where are they supposed to go from there? Many districts reduce or even eliminate observations for tenured teachers. Other schools stop checking for lesson plans altogether. After all, when individuals have achieved tenure—within the gestational period of an elephant—they are deemed "masters of their domain."

This is quizzically done in the name of professionalism. Yet what it tends to do is create educational echo chambers in which practitioners could, if they so desired, hear only one voice for the remainder of their careers: their own. This has the propensity to create tremendous barriers during periods of unprecedented change, like we are currently experiencing.

Of course, what true, awe-inspiring, life-affirming mavens of motivation and champions of chalk have learned over time is that there is no mountaintop. Mastery cannot be achieved. The closer you get, the more you realize how much you do not yet know and how much has profoundly changed since you first began acquiring your skills and interacting with children in a professional capacity.

This revelation inspires lifelong learning and the *pursuit* of mastery—a far cry from the fabricated construct of tenure and the antithesis of those whose lesson plans have turned yellow over the decades or are safely stored on their Office Max 4GB thumb drives.

Former Milwaukee Brewers manager Dave Bristol phrased this much more succinctly:

"There'll be two buses leaving the hotel for the park tomorrow. The two o'clock bus will be for those of you who need a little extra work. The empty bus will leave at five o'clock."

2. Diplomatic Immunity

As it turns out, nearly ironclad job protection can make some relatively rational people embrace considerably irrational behavior. Perhaps even more absurd than the actions themselves is the mentality that unprofessional actions should not be met with significant consequences. Or to put it another way, "I have tenure, so unless I hit a kid, there's nothing you can do to me." (Regrettably, that line was not made up.)

Of course, the majority of educators with tenure do not, nor would they ever, conduct themselves with such an air of diplomatic immunity. Unfortunately, some do and each of those individuals is responsible for educating children in a learning environment replete with dedicated colleagues and supervisors with whom they are expected, but often fail, to work collaboratively and productively. Isn't that something in need of remedy?

3. Horrible Bosses (Get Tenure) Too

As if a lifetime appointment for a highly ineffective classroom teacher were not disadvantageous enough, imagine the possible damage that can be wrought by a similarly maladroit administrator. Leaders who are short sighted, ill tempered, vindictive, and borderline megalomaniacal establish environments that dishearten well-intentioned teachers, diminishing the possibility they will take risks and rise to their given potential. This also fosters a "let me close my door and figure out my own thing" mindset because teachers have little recourse against a tenured principal and, understandably, fear reprisals.

Other bosses may play favorites, offering plum assignments to those who have taken loyalty oaths while the rest receive scraps from the table. Some supervisors may not know which end of the pencil to use, yet they are charged with decision making that impacts the future of children and the morale of professionals, who earnestly try to overcome the morass to make a difference.

These administrators are proof positive of Dr. Laurence J. Peter's "Peter Principle," which postulates that individuals rise to the level of their own incompetence. Leaders such as these do not deserve the protections that tenure affords.

4. Break Free the Chains

With the (unlikely) exception of a massive, bipartisan, nationwide commitment to repairing the torn social fabric of our society, which has produced tragic levels of income, educational, and opportunity gaps over the course of generations, the fastest way to better schools is to remove the shackles of tenure and let talent find talent. Performance reviews and observation rubrics are no match for educators who will vote with their feet. You will know who the effective teachers are because principals will clamor to hire them. And you will learn who the truly terrible leaders are by the stampede for the exits.

What better way to reward a wonderful teacher than to pair him or her with like-minded colleagues and an administrator who values his or her worth, inspiring him or her to be the best educator he or she can possibly be. What better bounty for leaders, who invest blood, sweat, and tears in their buildings, than to have the good fortune of engaging in meaningful and symbiotic relationships with those in their charge—professionals who will, in turn, challenge their bosses to be the best visionary leaders they can be. But talent has to be allowed to find talent rather than be tethered to the cinderblock of tenure.

Tenure provokes people to act irrationally, often in opposition of their personal interests. We see this with every talented, energetic teacher or administrator who feels unappreciated or burdened with his or her current placement but who will not seek a change because he or she does not want, or believes he or she cannot afford, to give up tenure. Such people are willing to sacrifice the potential of achieving long-lasting happiness to allay their short-term insecurities. That speaks to the emotional power of tenure, which cultivates irrational decision making. There is a very practical predicament that occurs as well.

Let us examine, for a moment, the lamentable reality of a truly spectacular teacher with fifteen years of experience who is seeking a change because her newly tenured principal is the love child of Caligula and Pol Pot. In a rational environment, such an educator would be highly sought after: seasoned, excellent track record, in her prime.

Thanks to tenure, however, that individual is practically unhireable. Her untouchable status does not stem from a lack of talent but rather the certainty that the payrolls of other school districts are clogged up by a handful of underwhelming, ineffective, tenured teachers they are unable to shed.

Like a person who remains in an unhealthy relationship for all of the wrong reasons, our superstar educator has no way out of her quagmire. Whether it is an unwillingness or an inability to escape from her predicament, over time the result is usually the same: contempt. This is one reason why tenure can be unfairly limiting for educators. On the other side of the spectrum we find individuals with whom tenure provides a sense of freedom or entitlement that is so absolute it can sprout behavior that borders on unprofessional or insubordinate.

One of the common refrains from the Educational Swiss Guard devoted to defending tenure is that, in its absence, teachers would be abused by tyrannical principals. However, it is the very protections granted by tenure that allow some principals to practice despotism. Without tenure, building administrators have *more* reason to treat hard-working teachers like gold. They would not want members of their staff to leave if for no other reason than their failure to galvanize the faculty would cost their own jobs.

Right now, only two facets really govern adult behavior in a school building: professionalism and morality. Merit pay, high-stakes tests, observations, and all other attempts at accountability are spitballs going up against the Great Wall of Tenure. Without tenure there would be incredibly powerful incentives to make professional relationships work on both ends of the equation. The result would be greater collegiality and collaboration, producing schools that maximize the human capacity of the adults responsible for inspiring and educating children.

Perhaps there was a time when tenure was a good idea. That time has passed.

Epilogue

In days of old, the school was always right and the mere whisper of a phone call home would cause student tremors. The pendulum has swung, as many of today's educators shudder when they hear a parent is calling the school. Likewise, nary a generation ago, a teacher could sit at his or her desk and command the light brigade. As long as books remained open, pencils were in motion, and silence pervaded the air, the classroom atmosphere was considered exemplary. The idle were considered idols. But no more.

Attention spans are shorter. Sitting still is nearly impossible for many students, especially young boys. Children now possess a constant craving of glowing screens that can be swiped. Learning styles have changed. And to make things even more difficult, the stakes of education have never been higher due to globalization and the ensuing evaporation of many industrial employment opportunities, which had provided decades of stable middle-class lifestyles for millions. And in a world that continues to move forward fast, the unlucky and uneducated are prime targets to be left behind. That makes the classroom ground zero.

Given their influence, classrooms need to be filled with positive, constructive energy from teachers and students. This begins with an injection of passion from the adults who set the tone. Children are incredibly proficient at detecting authenticity, so the passion for teaching and learning must be genuine. No matter how many devices may fill the room, they should never be permitted to obstruct meaningful human interaction. We would be well served if classroom teachers viewed their work as performance art.

Performance artists want to stir emotions and generate thought-provoking experiences for their audiences. They transform others by using sound and movement, not by sitting behind a desk. Viewing the delivery of instruction in this way will help educators infuse originality and heart into the many cookie-cutter curricula that are often mandated by states and school districts. Additionally, they will inspire multifaceted, emotional responses from their students.

Knowledge will be shared, but more importantly, fires will be lit.

With more and more learning software featuring artificial intelligence hitting the market, there is a serious risk that education will become colder and far more impersonal. Distance learning may truly make people feel distant. To mount a defense, we need dynamic and enthusiastic salespeople to peddle the greatest product of all time: a well-developed mind.

Teaching is an art. Be an artisan.

About the Author

Marc Isscks has been an educator for nearly twenty-five years, serving as a classroom teacher, department chairperson, content specialist, and building administrator over that span. He is a founder of the Nassau County Assistant Principals' Association in New York. Marc has published several articles on education and is currently a PhD student. For more information about the author and the Internet Ethics curriculum, visit marcisseks.com.